S0-ENU-808

A GOLDEN EAGLE STORY

How I Soared to Millions of Dollars in Sales

A GOLDEN EAGLE STORY

How I Soared to Millions of Dollars in Sales

By

Victor Babb

Edward D. Sargent, Editor

Duncan and Duncan, Inc., Publishers

Copyright © 1998 by Victor Babb

All rights reserved, including the right of reproduction in whole or in part in any form.

For ordering and/or distribution, contact:
Duncan and Duncan, Inc.
2809 Pulaski Highway, P.O. Box 1137, Edgewood, MD 21040
(410) 538-5579. Fax: (410) 538-5584. E-Mail: dunandpb@frontiernet.net

Edited by Edward D. Sargent

Graphic Design by Sargent Communications, Inc.
Desktop Publishing Division

Library of Congress Catalog Card Number: 98-70335

Printed in the United States of America

Library of Congress Cataloging-in-Publication Data:

Babb, Victor, 1944–
A Golden Eagle Story: How I Soared to Millions of Dollars in Sales

1. Insurance agent/broker — autobiography. 2. Afro-Americans in Business — Autobiography. 3. United States Citizen. 4. Education and Training; 5. Motivation. 6. How to.

ISBN 1-878647-51-2 abc

Victor Babb
Insurance Broker

One of the Top Insurance Salesmen in the World

Special Sales and Management Performance Awards Include:

No. 1 Allstate Agent
In Life Insurance Sales
The State of New York
1995

Life Millionaire Club Honoree
Life Leader's Club Honoree
9 Times

Honor Ring Honoree
15 Times

Allstate Quality Agent

Equitable Life National Management Citation Award
4 Times

In memory of my mother, Doris Theodore Babb, and to all the children around the world, regardless of race, creed, color, gender, nationality or religion, whose great potential deserves to be set free forever.

Contents

Foreword xi
By The Rev. Dr. Floyd H. Flake,
Former Six-Term U.S. Congressman (D-NY),
Pastor, The Cathedral of Allen A.M.E. Church, Queens, NY

Introduction xv

I. My Mother's Love: My Greatest Asset 1

II. "I Beg You, Do Not Quit!" 19

III. Turning Points 38

IV. Success Is a Mind Game 52

V. The ABCs: Always Be Closing 67

VI. The Sales Call 83

VII. Born to Win 105

VIII. Mr. Grandsouldt: An Eagle for All Seasons . . 120

IX. Soaring: From Continent to Continent 125

Foreword

Amidst the many changes that have occurred in American society over the past 30 years by virtue of government intervention in the lives of African Americans through programs that have made many feel a sense of dependency, it is refreshing to find someone like Victor Babb, who has succeeded the old fashioned way—through hard work, discipline and focus on self-initiative.

The roots of the African American experience are replete with stories of individuals who have literally pulled themselves up by their own bootstraps, even when their boots had holes in them. Victor joins this illustrious body of over achievers and through *A Golden Eagle Story* challenges today's youth, not merely by rhetoric, but by the power of his accomplishments, to believe that there is within them the power to achieve successes beyond their imaginations.

Victor understands the relationship between his successes and his family roots, exemplified by a mother who stood over her children "like a tree planted by the rivers of water." This story should be an inspiration for all mothers who are single parents, and who often fail to understand the power they have to be positive influences in the lives of their children. His remembrance of his mother's love, teachings on moral behavior and constant encouragement represent three principles worthy of emulation by any parent raising children in this era, which has been labeled "Generation X."

The book presents a compelling challenge with Victor's plea for all who are in pursuit of success to persevere and not quit, even when faced with adversity. One can feel his movements through the various levels and positions of his life as he reveals the trials of rising from the depths of newspaper entry level positions, through factory jobs, to the height of his profession as a top Allstate Insurance Company Agent. His is the story of victory snatched from the jaws of defeat and provides incentive for anyone wishing to overcome socioeconomic barriers and other restrictions that often defeat people in their pursuit of success.

From Victor's experiences in 1974 until today, as the rewards of his labor allow him to fly among the Eagles, he has demonstrated the dividends of his willingness to invest in himself through education and training. He argues by the example of his life that persons who are successful must believe in revelation and respond to the changes that it brings. Without revelation there is no vision, and without vision people perish, according to the scriptures.

Victor has made revelation and vision the hallmark of his successful pursuits. His willingness to focus on continuing education and new opportunities for personal growth and development has allowed his life to represent the best of the fulfillment of the American Dream of financial security and participation in the economic viability of this nation.

One of the most powerful segments of the book is the chapter entitled, "Success is a Mind Game." Here he challenges the reader to develop a sense of purpose by focusing on a life goal. It is remarkable that he moves beyond traditional definitions of the born leader to challenge ordinary people to follow in his footsteps through discipline and preparation for the great opportunities that await them. He makes a compelling argument to ordinary people by challenging them to always be ready to respond to the extraordinary circumstances that life presents, if they intend to succeed.

Readers will be able to see themselves sitting around the table with Victor and his friends talking about their future. The image of youths talking about and hoping for the future is powerful when contrasted against many youths who believe they will not live beyond their teen years.

This chapter also discusses the importance of the role model in his life, Robert Grandsouldt, whose positive mental attitude greatly impacted Victor. Modeling his life after Grandsouldt, Victor worked at grasping every facet of departmental operations, worked the jobs others would not do and toiled long hours.

As he worked, he was diligent in maintaining his integrity and honesty while projecting a sense of fairness by respecting everyone's opinion. He makes a compelling argument that everyone needs a person like Grandsouldt after whom to model his or her life.

The book also speaks of the ABCs, Victor's "Always Be Closing" philosophy, which undergirds his success as a salesperson and reflects the attitude individuals must have if they are to succeed in any profession. The principle of having knowledge of oneself and knowledge of others in a sales situation projects beyond the confines of the sales profession and is certainly a principle that has led to success in the lives of many people in all walks of life.

A Golden Eagle Story is the story of the life of a man who could have focused on the limitations of his immigrant background, but rather chose to take full advantage of the resources available to him in America—the land of opportunity.

A Golden Eagle Story is also the story of a man who dared to soar as high as he possibly could. Victor saw in America a paradise of uncultivated opportunities and decided to become an achiever who would break up the fallow ground of his mind in order to participate fully in the blessings of being a citizen of this great country.

A man of faith, guided by the power of the Holy Spirit, Victor Babb exemplifies the spirit of one with a committed heart and appreciation for his successes, yet possesses compassion and concern for the success of others, as evidenced through his commitment to share the attributes that have made him a Golden Eagle.

Readers cannot help but be moved to begin their own journeys towards success with the hope of concluding by writing their own Golden Eagle stories.

— The Rev. Dr. Floyd H. Flake
Former Six-Term U.S. Congressman (D-NY)
Pastor, The Cathedral of Allen A.M.E. Church, Queens, NY

Introduction

I wrote *A Golden Eagle Story: How I Soared to Millions of Dollars in Sales* because in my journey to perform at my very best I have discovered something great. I have discovered the Golden Eagle Spirit. I want to thank Ted C. Crews, my first insurance sales manager, for bringing out the Eagle in me. I also want to thank my niece, Brenda. I finally decided to write this book after she encouraged me to take on the challenge of becoming an author while I was vacationing in south Florida. Others have urged me to write also. The most poignant push forward came at the end of a sales seminar where I had spoken about my life in the insurance business. After I sat back down, my friend and fellow agent Freddie Siddall, who was seated beside me, whispered in my left ear: "Victor, you should write a book."

Please do not be misled by the cover or the title of this book. It is not only about being successful in sales. It is not just about the affairs of business. It is also about the affairs of your heart and soul. You see, the Golden Eagle Spirit empowers you to pursue any worthy goal your mind can conceive. It gives wings to your dreams, whatever they may be.

Therefore, it is my sincere hope that this book will move you out of your comfort zone and into many, new positive directions. I hope that it initiates or reinforces the belief that the Golden Eagle vision survives and thrives in America, the Caribbean, Europe, Africa, and Asia. All across the world, despite the controversies, bigotry, discord and confusion that often hinder individual freedom and achievement, dreams are born everyday. This book will help guide anyone willing to pursue a dream to mount up with wings and soar to the highest altitudes of success.

— Victor Babb

A GOLDEN EAGLE STORY

How I Soared to Millions of Dollars in Sales

I

My Mother's Love: My Greatest Asset

I migrated from Guyana, South America, to the United States on December 7, 1968. I arrived at New York City's John F. Kennedy International Airport in the late evening, carrying a small, dark blue, used suitcase, which was given to me for good luck by a friend. The only money that I had was a Guyanese ten dollar bill along with some loose change.

I was greeted at the airport by my sponsor, Daphne. She carried with her a tattered, oversized, black wool winter coat. As she handed the heavy coat to me, she said matter-of-factly, "You're in America, now. It's cold up here."

I took the coat and started walking out of the airport towards the taxi stand. There was one thing on my mind: my mother, Doris Babb. She was blessed with eight, healthy and strong children. I am the last of the bunch. She was married to the Rev. Cecil Fitzgerald Babb, assistant pastor of a Seventh Day Adventist Church.

Unbeknown to anyone in the family, I left Guyana on the same day as my sister. We had each planned our trips separately and quietly, like little squirrels preparing for winter. Suddenly, it came as a great surprise that we were booked on the very same Pan Am airplane bound for New York City.

My mother was heartbroken to know that not one, but two of her children were leaving on the same day and at the same time. Like her, I too was shocked to know that this was actually happening. I could tell that my mother did not know what to do or how to take this news.

Mother, who passed in early 1998, was a Bible-carrying woman. Wherever she went, she took her Bible. To the grocery store or to the doctor's office, she carried her Bible. I don't believe that she ever even tasted any alcohol. Perhaps she sneaked some wine or whiskey at some time or another. But, my eyes never saw her do it. Only recently did I learn that on the day that I and my sister, Pearl, traded Guyana for America, my mother had a strong drink to ease her pain. But, she did not get drunk. "Parting was truly hard," Mom said.

My mother and I had been through so much together when I was a boy. When I was seven years old, I was suddenly struck with a pain in my abdomen. Not totally believing in doctors, mother prayed for two days. She waited patiently to see whether God would answer her prayers and stop my suffering. Eventually, she decided to take me to Georgetown Hospital in Georgetown, British Guyana. I vividly remember the white English doctor advising my mother that he had diagnosed my symptoms as appendicitis. His next statement was, "If you had kept this boy home any longer, he would have ruptured on the inside and he could have died."

Within moments, I was rushed into the operating room. The entire procedure took about three hours. According to what I was told, I was in the hospital for almost another full day before I fully recovered from the anesthesia. While I lay in a bed in the children's ward, my cousin, Ena, who was a supervisor in the laundry room at the hospital, chipped in for my mother, coming to my bedside to pray when Mom could not come to visit and comfort me.

My love for my mother was magnified through the years. Many young people grow up today not knowing what a real mother's love is. Just look at the nightly news and you will soon agree with me.

My mother was 90 years old when she died. She was still very tough in mind, body and soul. Until the day she journeyed to the other side of this life, she engaged in lively discussions. She was and still is my "Golden Eagle" because she was so strong in her convictions and she always had a clear vision of what she wanted, where she wanted to go, and how she was going to get there.

During the last seven years of her life, my mother's conversations became pointedly direct. She once asserted, reflecting on her life as a mother: "I prefer to deal with the boys, not the girls. Give me the boys any day." For some reason, it seemed that she had made a final assessment of this matter. I don't quite know why she felt it was so important to say this, but I had always observed that, indeed, she had a strong affinity for young, aspiring men. When I visited Nigeria, I realized that it was a distinct African woman's trait to mold young men.

Mother was very assertive, yet liberal with her love. Some people would call this "tough love." I call it simply, Mother Eagle Love—the kind of love that empowers a mother to teach her eaglets the hard lessons of sacrifice and discipline while simultaneously sharing a warmth that engenders a sense of security and confidence. When I was three years old, my mother and father, who is also deceased, separated. I was too young to understand what was happening. So, my mother was both mother and father to me. At that time she had seven children to care for. My sister, Lucille, was left in Barbados to look after my father, who by then had been transferred there to be the pastor of his own church.

My mother loved to tell the story of her first visit to see my father in Barbados about two years before their separation. She took me with her in a small, shanty of a boat on October 9, 1945. I was less than a year old at the time and could not comprehend the danger we were in, but she later told me that the waves of the Atlantic ocean were much too high and rough for that journey in such a small vessel. However, she was hell bent on making this trip to join my father, who was also a painter, carpenter and first-class shoemaker. We arrived safely, but after my grandmother became sick back home in British Guyana, my mother was forced to make a return trip in that same small boat on October 2, 1948. She was determined that she and I would make it across the Atlantic one more time. As she later explained, this time the rough seas were joined by the hazardous high winds. When the two natural forces got together, there was a lot of tossing and turning going on.

"We were being tossed from side to side in that tiny boat," she told me. "The captain was shouting, again and again, 'Whoever can pray, pray!'"

They were trying to make it through a sudden storm. It was hurricane season. What a test of will and faith. My mother prayed with power and passion. Everyone aboard could feel her conviction. Today I thank God for hearing and answering my mother's prayers on that scary journey back home.

Years later, I returned home on a jet plane, far above the dangerous sea, to visit Mother for Thanksgiving. When she saw me, she exclaimed, "Victor, you are a gift to me from God."

What a lovely thing for a mother to say to her child. My older sister always says that my mother blessed me while she lived. The other siblings were not so fortunate. The others used to eat their hearts out because she referred to me as "the king," "the president," "the chairman" or "the leader" in all of her lengthy letters.

My other brothers and sisters grew weary because of this high honor given to me by our mother. After she became a senior citizen, I gladly took on the responsibility of making sure that her needs were met. Of course, this was a very small price to pay for all that she had done for me to enable me to survive and thrive on this planet.

Under the banner of my mother came the lessons of hard work and obedience. As a boy, I was allowed discretionary time to play outside and to go to the YMCA, just as long as I got on my hands and knees to wax the small living room and dining room floors of our house. In addition, I had to answer the alarm clock at 4:00 a.m. five times a week in order to report to the local daily newspaper's circulation department. There I was responsible for folding and delivering newspapers in order to help my mother put food on the table for me and my older brothers and sisters. My father did not send much money for the upkeep of his wife and children. This awful situation persisted for years.

After doing my normal early morning shift at the newspaper company, I reported to Saint James The Less Primary School in Kitty Village, where I was a member of the cricket team. After school, the team practiced for at least an hour. Many days after school, my mother would finish washing and pressing the English Army clothes for me to deliver. While delivering the cleaned clothes to the officers' residences, I picked up more dirty clothes for Mother to wash. I walked for miles, hitching a ride on a donkey cart, horse-drawn cart, or, if I was lucky, the drivers of the old English yellow bus would tuck me under the fare stile and I would take a seat in the back of the bus. I would feel so sorry for my mother, knowing that she had to work so damn hard for her children. Sometimes she would be up until 4:00 a.m. when I left to deliver the newspapers. She would work all day and night washing by hand, ironing, baking or sewing.

Hers was a normal life among the poor. She had so few possessions, but was rich in faith. From my young vantage point, I saw her keeping the faith and fighting a good fight. The most devastating time I experienced with my mother was during the British Guyana civil disruption that escalated into the worst riots in the country's history. The upheaval began in February 1961 and lasted until 1964. There were hardly any jobs, food or supplies in the country. My mother would watch and pray by day and night. As the wife of a Seventh Day Adventist pastor, she obeyed the doctrine of the church. I never looked forward to Friday afternoon because after 6:00 p.m., there would be no cooking or eating until sundown Saturday.

Two years after the disturbances made their mark, British Guyana gained her independence from England. On May 26, 1966, the country became a republic, with 83,000 square miles of land at its disposal. The name of the country was changed to

Guyana. The country's population was approximately 834,000.

Guyana had been lacking in development for more than 150 years while being under colonial rule. It was pillaged, raped and exploited by the British. It was divided and dominated by the rich expatriates.

Throughout the civil unrest and hardships that it brought, I was confused as to what was going on. I was still a child. Nevertheless, I never complained and I never gave my mother any trouble whatsoever. That is not to say that I did not do the things that little boys do. Of course, I did. But, I knew where to draw the line. I knew my mother truly expected me to be a good son. I knew she was protecting me from life's turmoils as much as possible, so that I could grow up balanced and sure of myself. She knew something special was going to happen to me in my life.

When I reached the age of 12, my mother told me that the midwife who was present at my birth made a prediction. She said, "This baby is long and thin, with bright eyes. He looks like a leader." So, I suppose from birth, my mother was grooming me to assume the role of leadership. She used to tell this story over and over.

She also loved to tell the story of why she named me Victor. Saddled with seven children at the time, she was pregnant with me when her husband was leaving for Barbados, but she did not tell him. She was frightened by the thought of bringing another child into this world. Obviously, her marriage to Rev. Cecil Babb was in some trouble. She tried to commit suicide, but she failed. With pride and thankfulness, she later said, "I was hanging on to the Blood of Jesus Christ." There was just so much pressure on her with all of the children and a sickly mother depending on her to take care of their every need everyday.

The doctor gave Mother a choice while she was in labor. It was her or I. One of us had to die due to complications. She decided to give me the chance to live. What bravery! She put her own life on the line for me. Deep within she believed that all would be well for both of us despite the medical prognosis. Yet, there was a chance that she would not make it to the other side of her ordeal.

Can you imagine 48 hours of labor? That would be enough for any mother to give up and throw in the towel. She already had seven children and did not want another. She had concealed her pregnancy from my father, so if she had decided to let me go, he would have never known. She had every excuse she needed to escape the pain. Yet, she persevered and we both made it to the other side of that severe trial and tribulation. You can surely appreciate that it was a larger-than-life victory for her when she saw her baby boy for the first time.

"I was victorious, so I named you Victor," she said. "You represented victory."

My mother's younger brother, a policeman, predicted that I would be a great young man. So, he came up with the name Alexander, after the king of Macedonia, Alexander the Great, for my middle name.

My mother always pushed me to be the best. By the time I became a teenager, I was one of the best school cricketers and soccer players. I was also a YMCA table tennis champion and captain of the dominos team. Then I did something really special. Joining the Sea Scouts was a giant step up for me. It was a high rung on the ladder to manhood.

I was already involved in so many other things, such as

playing sports, delivering newspapers and helping my mother with her cleaning jobs. I also visited on a regular basis various construction sites with her and my eldest sister, Elva, to help sell lemonade and other refreshments. Yet, despite the distractions and obligations, I was determined to wear the handsome uniform and the beautiful badges of the Sea Scouts. Similar to the Boy Scouts, the naval-oriented Sea Scouts required youngsters to perform various tasks and duties in order to advance within the ranks. The Sea Scouts were very popular in England, and Guyana, being under British rule, adopted this tradition. After nine months of dedicated service, I became a troop leader.

My dear mother had all of this love and care that she was putting into the preparation for other peoples' clothes. So, of course, she wanted to see her baby boy well pressed and suited up in his Sea Scout navy blue and white uniform. I led many parades and was always out front as the English Governor reviewed the troops during huge ceremonial parades down main street. Mother was always there waving with outstretched arms. "Vic! Vic! I see you!" she'd yell.

As a Sea Scout I had to exercise the discipline and commitment of a soldier. The flag had to be hoisted at precisely 1800 hours every Friday. Other chores were also mandatory. Being ever watchful and alert was a must. The high point of my scouting days occurred during one late Friday evening in August 1961. I was on my way home from scout practice when I noticed a small crowd gathering near a lake. I heard somebody shouting, "There's a man overboard! Man overboard!" I immediately pulled off my perfectly pressed uniform and jumped into the lake.

I brought the inebriated man out alive. He was breathing unevenly and going through spasms. His lungs were filled with water. Sadly, he finally succumbed on his way to the hospital. Word of my rescue attempt spread quickly and the authorities gleefully awarded me my first Sea Scout Medal of Bravery. The next day's headlines read, "Sea Scout Tries to Save Drowning Man."

I would have never jumped into the lake and tried to pull a grown man out of the water if the Sea Scouts had not taught me how to swim. Still, it was my mother who inspired me to learn how to swim. One of her favorite sayings was "Always be ready to swim because, boy, one day you might have to swim for your life."

Mother used to say things like that all of the time. Another of her favorites was: "Show me the company you keep and I'll tell you who you are." On character, she said: "It must be good enough to inspire a parade." On power, she said, "Power must be earned, or touch the wire and get shocked."

Of all of her intriguing sayings, the one that I best remember is this: "Life is like electricity. If you want the power, you have to flip the switch." I understood this to mean that you have to do something in order to get something. You have to turn something on—turn on your mind, turn on your inner power, turn on your ideas, turn on your physical strength. Flip that switch and go get what it is you really want in life. Too many people lose out in life because they just don't flip that switch and turn on their God-given power.

I flipped the switch in the wrong way once and ended up embarrassing my mother for the first and only time in my life. I was working at a consumer goods company called Sandbach

Parker. I bought a wonderful, lime green, nine-cubic-foot Kelvinator refrigerator for her on a lay a way plan. I recall not paying for it for a two-month period. One day I went home for my lunch break. Much to my surprise, the company was waiting there to recover the refrigerator. I was never so hurt for my mother. She didn't seem too upset because she knew that I was trying in my own little way to help her save the leftover meals for the next day. As a lad, it was always in my heart to see my mother not wanting nor in need. However, from that moment on, I made the decision that never again would I ever subject my mother to such humiliation.

"Money gives you power, but you have to know how to place it," Mother told me gently. "Some people have mouth power, but their works prove who has the real power." My mouth had written a check that my wallet couldn't cash.

I dug in at work and tried to sell as many consumer goods as possible so that I could earn enough money to have the kind of power needed to buy things and keep them, instead of worrying about how to keep up the payments.

I thought about my absent father. All these years had gone by and he was still in Barbados trying to save souls. Meanwhile, Mom was trying desperately to make ends meet. Just to save a dime, she would walk home five miles after leaving her Chinese laundry job every day.

It was expected, back in those days, for the mother to be a matriarch—the rock solid anchor of the home. She was expected to provide for her young children. Looking back, however, I am convinced that Mother worked so tirelessly not just to be the strong matriarch, but also to preserve her sanity.

Sheila, a very dear friend of my mother, used to tell her

that "Victor will be the one to take care of you one day." All of my life I grew up thinking that surely it would be my responsibility to take care of my mother.

Mother loved to entertain friends who would drop in to see her. Since she and her children celebrated the Sabbath on Saturday and Sunday was a rest day, folk would drop by on weekends just to chat and chill with her. Sitting at the small kitchen table, Mother and her friends would talk, laugh and sing together for hours. Mother would bake bread and cakes for them. They would always pray and have a church session right there in the kitchen. Mother would say, "The stars go in, the moon goes in, but they all come back out. Let us be strong and of good courage."

When I was 14, my mother wrote to my father asking him to support my efforts in school. He refused. She later told me that the only thing she could then do was pray to God that I would become the man I am today. Still, my mother said, I am like my father. "He was no fool. He always had two keys and three pennies in his pocket." He was poor, but you would have thought that he had money, she said.

My mother said that her back was to the wall, with all those children and no man at home. It often seemed that we hardly had enough food to eat. She tried to prevent any infighting among the children by telling us to "keep your eyes on your own plate. Eating time is a happy time, so be glad with what you have."

My mother was committed to keeping people calm. She was an excellent peacemaker and would have made the perfect diplomat. She would tell us all of the time: "If you do not have a destructive mind, the peace of God will reign inside of you. The Holy Spirit will dwell within."

It seems to me that my mother's primary purpose in life was to keep her children together and to love Christ. She certainly fulfilled her mission, for all of her children continue to stay close to each other and to God and they treat others like human beings.

Ephesians 6:1-3 says: "Children, obey your parents in the Lord; for this is right. Honor thy father and mother; which is the first commandment with promise; That it may be well with thee, and thou mayest live long on the earth."

I realize that there are some things that money just can't buy. One is my mother's love: my greatest asset.

Mother's lot in life was to do hard work and not to win the lottery, yet I knew that God would bless her with a long life because she took care of children whether they were hers or not. Her ideals are summed up in a song entitled "If I Can Help Somebody," which was broadcasted every day at 3:00 p.m. in Guyana while I was growing up. It was played during a gospel program on Radio Demerara. God help us if the old English power plant had shut down while that song was on the air. My mother would have had a fit if she couldn't sit by the radio and hear these words by songwriter A. Bazel Androzzo: "If I can help somebody as I pass along; if I can cheer somebody with a word or song; if I can show somebody he is traveling wrong, then my living shall not be in vain . . . If I can do my duty as a Christian ought; if I can bring back beauty to a world up-wrought; if I can spread love's message that the Master taught, then my living shall not be in vain."

My mother taught by example. She taught me how to pray and to count my blessings. She taught me how to have faith. She taught me how to survive and how to always be lively. My mother told me that God is King and He is the only one to fear.

Today I rejoice in my mother's everlasting love and in her wisdom. She told me to "stand tall in all you do because if you fall, getting back up is hard to do." She instilled this in me and life has reinforced it. Yes, I know now that it is truly much better to keep standing and to not risk making foolish mistakes. But if you do fall, it's how you get back up that counts.

I have tried hard not to disappoint my mother. She shielded me from all of the problems in her life so I could be free to spread my wings and branch out. Sometimes in my mind I say, "Mother, I am flying high now, soaring like an eagle, number one in my field, selling millions of dollars of insurance a year. Wow, can you see me? Can you see me now? Thank you for saving me from death itself, so I could live like this!"

What a powerful inspiration it is to have a mother like her. I believe that most of us have a mother or father or someone in our lives who truly loves us the way my mother loved me. Perhaps that special someone does not express it, but the love is there in the works he or she does. It is important to appreciate this kind of person in your life. It is critical to success to appreciate those people who help you.

It is also important to be mindful of your enemies as well. Don't let them get too close. Mother told me: "Not everyone will like you; not everyone will try to help you." She said, "Always find out who is in charge and go to that person to get what you want. Get your permission, your pardon, your peace and your power from the one who is in charge. You will get messed up with subordinate people who claim to have ultimate authority."

She said that some people are confused and will try to

confuse you likewise. She stressed that some people are insecure and will make life difficult for you. Some people have sick egos, so always watch and pray. She said, "Son, you must get to the top to make life uncomplicated for yourself." As a young man I never understood fully what she was trying to tell me. But, I never second guessed her advice. I wanted to know what the top felt like and now I know: It is *really* cool up here!

Because of my understanding of what the Lord did for my mother, I have signed onto that same market of faith. I have seen the days when she had nothing to give her children to eat and she had a question mark on her face. But somehow, because of her testament of hope, that question mark was soon turned into an exclamation mark. Again and again she has told me not to entrust my soul in any person's hands lest it be God Himself. "Go to the top!"

She was so eloquent. Her graying hair accented her dark complexion. Her pearly white smile and high cheek bones highlighted her rapidly moving jaw. She captivated anyone within hearing distance. Her bottom line testimony was simple: "When I had no friends, no money, no job, no friendly neighbors, a no-good boss, and no hope, no faith, and no shelter . . . When the doctor couldn't help me, I went to Jesus in secret prayer. I knew that He would make a way . . . When you must win, don't gamble. Do not be fooled by false authorities. Do not fall for false claims and false answers, such as cigarettes, alcohol, gambling, drugs, and two-bit hustlers. Hold your standards high. Don't do everything that comes into your mind. Examine it; pray over it; twist it and turn it over and over again and again. Test it and test it until you are absolutely certain that it is the correct decision for you to make."

My mother may not have been born with a silver spoon in her mouth, but she had gold in her heart. In her heart there was power. She taught me to love success and ambition. As a result of absorbing her determination and insight, I can assure you that neither your color nor education is a guarantee for your intelligence or success. My mother did not go to college, but I'm certain she could have run rings around any CEO. Even in her old age, she could tell you whether a lawyer had proven his case beyond a reasonable doubt. She had a master's degree from the college of hard knocks and a Ph.D. in faith.

It seems that God always gives His power to the weak, the underclass and the powerless. It is God's Affirmative Action Plan at work. He favors the meek, the humble and the peacemaker, for they will see Him and they will inherit the earth, according to the scriptures.

I was delighted to walk with my mother down the aisle of her church for communion on a Sunday a few weeks before Christmas 1996 while visiting her in the Caribbean. As we walked, she seemed to be as light as a feather, yet as solid as a rock. Later, at dinner, I looked her squarely in her eyes and asked, "What is the essence of your strength? What is the secret to your long life?"

She replied, "Wait your turn, then you'll know."

What kind of mother is this? A great mother. Her presence was simply awesome.

After a nail-biting life in her native land, Mother spent her retirement living in the eastern Caribbean island of Antigua. She reaped the benefits of her sweat, blood and tears. Our family built her a three-bedroom home to enjoy for the remainder of her blessed life. The brand new refrigerator purchased for her was never taken away, for the bill was paid in full.

Shortly after my mother moved into the house, my sister, Lucille, dedicated this poem to her:

Mother's Love Is Special

Mother's love is special,
Sometimes hard to explain
She is always there to love us again, again and again

An Angel she is; she guards and daily keeps
In her the love of God is what we see
When we need help her kindness is free

We thank God for her being here
For Mother is faithful and for our daily needs she cares

Seven of her children reside abroad, but they were always as close as her telephone, which was anchored on a small table next to her bed. We tried to convince her to live in North America. Of course, we failed. Mother preferred to stay in the Caribbean, where the average temperature is 85 degrees. She loved to worship her God and eat freshly prepared meals every day. I am sure that this was a big reason for her longevity. She adopted the same eating habits of her mother, who lived to be 76, and her grandmother, who lived to be 90.

Recently, Mom was called upon in church to testify. She eased her thin body up from the pew. Taking her time, she said firmly, "Because of His wonderful grace, that He has kept me onto now, I have no regrets. All the regrets are in me myself, but not with God. This morning I am happy to say that He is not finished with me, yet. No, He is not finished with me, yet. I still have work to do . . . And this morning, I am grateful for the prayers that have ascended to the throne of grace that my presence is here accompanied by my son, Victor, who has come back to be by my side. So, this morning, I give God all the praises and glory that He may keep me in the same way, for Jesus's sake, Amen."

With such a powerful mother as this, who would not be thinking of her at every momentous occasion of one's life? I have her on my mind every time I score a major victory or close an especially challenging sale.

I certainly gave God and Mother big thanks when I first stepped foot onto the precious soil of this land of freedom called America. I know that my Creator and my mother often worked hand in hand—He in his awesome omnipotence and her in her humble prayers—to shower blessings of opportunity upon me. This book is my best effort to share those blessings with others, so that they, too, might be blessed.

The foundation of any successful life is love—love of God, love of self and love of that special person or persons who sacrificed so that dreams could be born and pursued and success could be created. I thank my mother for revealing this great secret to me.

II

"I Beg You: Do Not Quit!"

As Daphne and I walked out of JFK Airport and into the blustery cold that fateful morning, December 7, 1968, a frozen, invisible hand slapped us in our faces. I quickly put on the winter coat that she had given me.

There was no problem catching a taxi and before I could say, "Well, here I am," we were in uptown Manhattan on 116th street, where my older brother, Gordon, had an apartment. As the taxi burrowed through traffic, I marveled at the many interesting-looking, high-rise buildings. Silently, I prayed for God's blessings and thanked Him and my mother for helping me to safely enter this new land of opportunity. I thanked them from the east, west, north and south of my heart. Without their help I might have ended up in some Amen corner, languishing in the shadows of my father's religious doctrine.

I turned to Daphne and thanked her, too. I had met her shortly before leaving Guyana. She was visiting Georgetown, Guyana from the United States and was browsing in Sandbach Parker, the business district of Georgetown, while I was trying to sell refrigerators. We became instant friends. When she returned to the U.S., she kept her promise and mailed me the immigration I-20 forms that I needed in order to obtain a student visa from the American Embassy in Georgetown. I was able to secure the two necessary affidavit of support letters from my Uncle Francis and a man I knew only as Mr. Clark, an insurance agent, who I had only met once before. With these important documents in hand, I was prepared to make my American journey.

My small suitcase was so tiny, I was able to hold it neatly on my lap as the cab maneuvered through the New York streets towards my brother's house. Gordon had gotten away from the pack when he was 17. He was now 27. When he greeted me, his eyes lit up like he had seen a vision. He was overjoyed that one of his own had also made the trek from Guyana. "Welcome to America, little brother! My home is your home."

I lived with Gordon for a week before he took me to an employment agency in New York City, which helped me to find a small factory job on Mott Street in Chinatown. This laborious job allowed a measly thirty minutes for lunch, but paid $70 per week. That was plenty of money in those days. I saved just about every penny and by Christmas I had enough to buy and ship gifts in a barrel to all of my family members.

Though the money at my new job was good, the work was lousy. The factory manufactured barbecue grill parts. I thought this job was a waste of my time because the work was not mentally stimulating. I just felt out of place there. My pride told me that I could do much better, for, to me, that factory job did not represent the American Dream. So, I quit after three weeks and searched for a new and better job, which I quickly found.

The months flew by and within a year I was not only making more money, I was also attending night school at Manhattan Community College, where computer programming was getting really hot. It was 1970 and the instructors were talking about computers as though they would be the biggest thing since sliced bread. Of course, now we know that the computer instructors were right on the money.

One of the computer programs I learned allowed me to calculate complex series of numbers. One day I punched in some figures from the historical $24 purchase of Manhattan from the Native Americans. The question I had for my IBM 1407 was this: "What would Manhattan be worth today at compound interest of nine percent since the purchase?" The answer was astounding. The computer almost ran out of digits.

My new job was in the famous New York City garment district. I worked at Chelsea Sports Wear as a packer. I was an instant hit with everyone there. Nat Cohen, the president of the company, would always make fun of my British accent. He called me "the Englishman." Eventually, his partner Herby, the presser Cordy, the floor manager, and everybody else also started referring to me as the Englishman.

On this job, I was able to pick up a bit of Spanish. Jimmy, my packing associate from Panama, would take his time to coach me. I enjoyed this very much. When the mostly Spanish-speaking messengers would come to pick up their merchandise, I would practice my Spanish lesson for the day on them.

It was at this job site that I developed a great appreciation for doing everything as though it had to be done yesterday. Murry, the cigar-smoking supervisor, would not hesitate to use an expletive if Jimmy and I could not finish packing merchandise for the UPS truck on time. To this day, when I see a UPS truck, I get speed in my feet and hands. Jimmy and I nicknamed UPS "Urgent Please, Sir."

My coworkers encouraged me to continue going to school. I remember Miss Mary, the seamstress, telling me, "Boy, I am proud of you foreigners. You all come here and get what you want." She and the other people I worked with were very inquisitive of me all of the time. I guess I was a novelty. Lisa, the bookkeeper, was the first white woman to kiss me on my cheek. She would hug me and kiss me like I was her son each time she saw me. This was before sexual harassment became a sore bone of contention in the workplace.

This was also before foreigners in the workplace were looked at with suspicion. So, though I did not have my permanent residency visa (green card), it didn't matter. In those days you could say that you were a citizen and get away with it.

After awhile, it was time to move on to greater opportunity. The way I found my next job was pretty interesting. One very cold day, I went to the fourth floor at 1372 Broadway, smiled and greeted the receptionist at Marlene Industries, where I was hopeful that I could get a job. The receptionist paged someone.

Suddenly, Jack appeared. He introduced himself as the personnel officer. I said to Jack: "If you let me work here starting today, Tuesday, I will work until Friday for free! By that time, sir, you will know how you like my work and, if you do not like my work, you do not have to pay me."

He quickly walked me down the corridor to the piece goods department and asked John to let me help him out until Friday and to report back to him about my performance. Each day I ate my lunch at my desk so that I could keep working. This impressed the company very much. By the end of the week, I was hired. I really enjoyed the work and John turned out to be one of the nicest bosses I have ever had. We still stay in touch from time to time.

John's assistant, Rich, was a brilliant young man with a master's degree in political science. I quickly learned everything I could from him about the clothing business. Rich was passionate about reading the Wall Street Journal for political stories. He also loved to tell me weird jokes and quiz me on the capital cities throughout the world.

Rich was totally amazed at what happened to me three months after joining the company. John, the supervisor, was leaving the industry and recommended me to the president to succeed him. The entire company was shocked by this decision. Rich was flabbergasted. Who was I to get this position over others who had been there way before me?

Monty, another good friend of mine, also from Guyana, was also made a supervisor with the company. We were the only two black people in any kind of supervisory roles there.

I worked closely with another manager, Lenny, who called me "Sidney Poitier." Bruce, another manager, used to call me "Harry Belafonte." This name would stick and very soon everyone would be calling me Belafonte, because of my husky, lyrical accent and my long sideburns.

Monty and I received promotion after promotion at Marlene Industries. We hired as many qualified Guyanese who applied for jobs with this company. There were countless.

Working in the garment district, especially at Marlene

Industries, and later at Elco Coat Company as assistant to the V.P., really sharpened me in terms of dealing with people and thinking on my feet. The jobs were demanding and stressful, but quite rewarding nevertheless. There were times when I wanted to quit, but I kept going. The contacts and skills I learned at those jobs helped me to step upwards years later, which goes to show you that you really never know how important a particular job is going to be in your life. That's why you should do your best and learn as much as you can from any opportunity that comes your way. For, tomorrow will depend on what you do today.

In 1973, I enjoyed a year's stay at Prime Envelopes Company in Newark, N.J. as an expediter. An expediter helps in the fulfillment process of filling orders for products. I left work each day at 4:30 p.m. in order to fight rush hour traffic in my 1967 Volvo and arrive in Secaucus, N.J. an hour later to work my night job at a fabric manufacturing company where I was a night manager.

Many of the workers were Hispanic, so the Spanish that Jimmy Houston taught me came in very handy there. I supervised as many as 24 Spanish-speaking people, who operated the dry-cleaning machines. The work there was not very difficult for me or the workers. My only responsibility was to be certain that all of the orders given to me by Steve, the general manager, were completed by midnight. I can vividly remember listening to the Watergate hearings, which investigated President Nixon's administration, on a small pocket radio while the Spanish people were working and talking among themselves. There was no stress in that job, let me tell you.

Still, I would get home to my Riverside apartment sometime

after 1:00 a.m. as tired as a work horse. I was hoping that my dear mother would be saying a prayer for me, as I wanted to get out of this harried, two-job situation.

In retrospect, being in New York, the core of the American melting pot, and working among the Jews, the African Americans, the Hispanics and the Chinese, gave me a good understanding of why the Lord created so many diverse races. It is required of all of us to accommodate and adapt ourselves to all of the races, especially when you have to work with them or interface with them as associates.

By 1974, I had worked for four American companies and had attended night school. My mind was now beginning to focus on a career that would pay me some seriously big cash.

Back in the old country, I always admired the successful insurance salesmen around town. I would see them wearing the best threads. They drove the best cars and lived in the best homes. They also had the most pretty women in town. They ate at the finest restaurants and went to the most expensive balls and parties. The politicians seemed to know them on a first-name basis. These guys always seemed to have money in their pockets, whether it was their money or not, unlike my father, who carried nickels and pennies.

I remember Les Wharton, Tony Michael and Peppi Romalo, just to name a few, who were big hitters back home in the insurance business. They seemed unstoppable. A famous Guyanese bicyclist, Percy Boyce, became Mr. Insurance. I had never thought in my wildest dreams that I would end up as a heavy hitter myself, excelling as an insurance broker in the United States of America.

Exactly how do you become a big success in your chosen

field? Let me say this here and now: somebody has to like you. I know this because somebody in the insurance business had to give me "the big break." Regardless of what you want to venture into, just hope that somebody likes you enough to show you the ropes.

You may learn your skills on your own or in school or on the job. But, more likely than not, you will need to grab somebody's coattails to really excel. For instance, it was my mother who taught me how to sell. She started me out selling buns and cakes, pots and pans, flowers and dolls. This gave me the foundation for what was to come.

To this day, I still give credit to Mom. I'll tell my associates, "America gave me a lot, but no one in America taught me how to sell. It was my mother who taught me how to turn anything into money." Whenever I go to a sales training seminar, I nod my head in appreciation for those hard-knock days as a child growing up without a father, under my mother's wing, learning how to deal with people and products.

The person who led the way to my receiving my big break in insurance was Bertram. He asked his friend, insurance agent Cecil, from Equitable Life Assurance Society of the United States, to join us for lunch one day during my tenure at Prime Envelopes in Newark. It was April 1974. We all met at a restaurant inside of the Robert Treat Hotel.

Cecil pitched me to buy a life insurance policy from him. He tried very hard, but I did not bend. He said that I would really help him out, if I signed up. I remember telling him that I had all of the insurance I needed. Actually, I really did not have any type of personal insurance, only what the job provided. At any rate, instead of Cecil selling me, he ended up sizing me up for a career with his company. He decided to take me under his wing. He must have seen the eagle in me.

The following week I was able to secure an appointment with Cecil's District Sales Manager (DSM), Ted Crews, who instantly liked me and offered me a career with his company. I filled out an application and was hired. Ted gave me some insurance industry books to study. I hit those books and I hit them hard. I did not waste any time with this new opportunity because those books were intended to prepare me to pass the New York State examination for life insurance agents.

I attended daily classes and every free moment I had I read and reread the material and completed the practice tests. There were moments when I wanted to throw those books over the Brooklyn bridge, yet something within me gave me the strength to persevere. Again, the hard work paid off and I was so happy when on my first attempt I passed the big life insurance exam.

Shortly after I received my results, I signed a contract with Equitable Life. It was June 1, 1974. My timing was perfect. I had the entire month to qualify for my first trip as an Equitable Life sales achiever. The company had started the monthly sales contest the previous February. Winners of the June contest would be treated to a stay at the historic Lake George Hotel and Resort in upstate New York.

I wanted to get my new career off with a bang, so I used the contest as a special incentive to push my enthusiasm into overdrive. I nearly touched the sky when I learned that I had won the trip.

My excitement was chilled, however, when I returned from the trip and was sternly reprimanded by the agency manager. He said that he was upset because I had invited a female guest to accompany me on the trip. After having a great time at Lake George, I was given this heartbreaking news. Though my female guest had stayed in another room, the manager chastised me as if I had committed a federal crime. Most of the other winners were married and, of course, invited their spouses.

This treatment did not sit well with me. It made me so angry that I even considered quitting just out of spite. I wanted to express my anger and relieve my frustration. However, ultimately, I decided that the smart thing was to channel my angst in a positive direction. So, I decided to get even with him by outperforming all of the Developing Sales Force Agents (agents with less than four years of service).

It was at this time that I developed certain sales tactics and strategies that I spell out in detail in a later chapter of this book (Chapter Five: "The ABCs: Always Be Closing"). I would pump myself up every night, praying fervently for God to show me countless opportunities to make successful sales attempts and give me the strength to capitalize on them. Thus, from the start of my career, I developed a habit of using the power of prayer to prepare myself to excel as a salesman.

I thank God that I did not sulk or become bitter as a result of my run-in with that arrogant agency manager. By working my butt off to shame him with my success, I stayed on the high road. My efforts were tiring, for sure, but my plan worked beautifully. I became the youngest top agent for that year and won a trip to San Francisco. What other agents had needed a year to do I accomplished in just six months.

My success made me hungry for more of the same. I looked for opportunities to sell everywhere I went. My heels were solidly dug into the sales game. Selling insurance became a way of thinking and a way of life.

I was blessed to have Ted Crews on my side. He wanted me to be a big success because once I did, he would reap great benefits as well. So, he worked diligently to help me master the insurance business.

On March 10, 1975, Equitable Life held its annual awards banquet at Leonard's of Great Neck, Long Island. I was officially named the 1974 Young Agent of the Year. This little boy from Georgetown, Guyana was now well on his way.

One of the agents, Anthony, chose a very touching way of showing the guests how much he admired what I had done as a young agent. He took off his velvet-trimmed, mohair jacket and spread it on the floor for me to step on as I ascended the dais. Two other agents and one of the sales managers got up from their seats and stood beside him. Then, they all saluted me. The audience laughed and applauded. I was so elated.

As I humbly received the accolades and the award, I realized that all of the studying and sacrificing and all of the cold calling and late-night appointments had paid handsome dividends. I gave a short speech, my first speech in the United States.

I had invited two special guests, Mr. and Mrs. Allen, to join me at the awards banquet. Since I was now a big shot, I sent a long, white, stretch limousine for their convenience.

I was proud to present to Mrs. Allen a bouquet of flowers. She certainly deserved this small honor, for she was my first sale and she gave me a list of 23 more people to contact. I had coldcalled Mrs. Allen, having obtained her name and number from a saleswoman who was trying to interest me in buying pots and pans. Mrs. Allen had been one of her contacts and the woman kindly shared this information with me.

When I made the appointment with Mrs. Allen on that sunny Saturday in June 1974, she gave me the following warning over the telephone: "Mr. Babb, your appointment is for 12:00 noon. You salesmen are always late for your appointments. If you are late, I will not see you. Do not bother to ring my bell."

She spoke with a squeaky, soft Bermudan accent, but she was very firm. I am glad she warned me, because during those hustling-to-make-it-to-the-top days, I would schedule my appointments two hours apart. Typically, my sales calls would include the presentation, a tea break and travel time. But, on the day of my appointment with Mrs. Allen, I scheduled nothing before noon. I wanted to be absolutely sure that I would arrive on time. I had my fingers crossed that my used car, which I had purchased only weeks before joining the Equitable company, would not let me down.

I was living on Riverside Drive in uptown Manhattan and I was unfamiliar with the neighborhood where she lived in Brooklyn. Since punctuality was the key word for the day, I left my home early in order to allow for lost time. I arrived in her block at 11:45 a.m., just to be sure that I could find the exact location of her house. At high noon on the dot I rang her door bell.

"You are the first salesman I ever met who came on time for an appointment," she remarked. She was starting to be sold already.

Within an hour, the sale was made and my very first family plan insurance policy was sold. We had an instant affinity for each other that lasted for years. In fact, eight years later, I was asked to be the master of ceremony for her choir director's

10th anniversary celebration. Her husband, Teddy, worked at Chock Full o' Nuts coffee shop. He too climbed aboard my bandwagon and was soon giving me names to call on as well. On Mrs. Allen's list was a lady by the name of Vera McCoy. She had a son, who was only 17 years old, but weighed 320 pounds! She was concerned that he might pass before she did. But, lo and behold, a couple of weeks after she had bought two life insurance policies from me—one for him and one for her—she was found slumped in her La-Z-Boy™ chair. Ms. McCoy was dead for three hours before anybody realized that she was gone.

This was my first death claim. Yvonne, my secretary, did not know how to break the news to me. It was not until years later that I heard one of Equitable's top agents say in a speech, "You are not an insurance agent until you have your first death claim." I knew what he was talking about because from the moment I learned that Vera McCoy was deceased, I treated every new sale that I made as if it would be my next death claim. In other words, to this day, I take the sale of a life insurance policy extremely seriously—as serious as a heart attack.

Shortly after I was presented the Equitable Life Young Agent of the Year Award, the agency manager said that he was so pleased with my performance that he was going to promote me to serve as one of his top assistants. The new position carried the title of Assistant District Sales Manager. A district consisted of a group of 10 or more sales agents.

A year later, I was given full DSM status. During each of the subsequent four annual periods, from 1975 - 1978, I won either Equitable's coveted Gold or Silver National Management Citation Award. I won each award twice.

Each award came with a star on a plaque. So, I guess I was sort of an insurance army four-star General. An old Guyanese friend of mine, Vincent, who had worked with me at the newspaper company back home, was very instrumental in my rapid ascension.

Vincent had moved to Brooklyn and was looking for a career. He was a printer by trade. After I learned that I was going to be promoted to DSM, I contacted Vincent to see whether he would be interested in joining me. I made an appointment to see him with his wife on Rutland Road in Brooklyn. During those days it was mandated that you interview an agent and his spouse in their home. The objective was to inspect the way they lived and to show courtesy to the spouse. I was able to convince his wife, Megan, that I would take good care of Vincent, her and their growing family.

Vincent joined me on the same day that I was officially promoted to DSM. He had no driver's license, much less a car. So, I showed him the ropes, just as Ted had done for me. Vincent excelled tremendously.

The Equitable agency where I worked was operated by a tough and strict business manager. In that environment, I grew stronger as a leader. In each of my first four years of management experience at Equitable Life, I developed one of my superstar agents into a DSM.

Sadly, another one of my Guyanese newspaper buddies, John, was too late for me to help him. I had not seen him for years. It was during one of my visits back to the old country that I spotted him riding an old, broken-down bicycle. He told me that he had moved to the U.S., but got cold feet and returned home. He quit on his dream. He could not believe that I was now in a position of power and could hire him. If he had stayed in America and called upon me for help, he would have been hired and groomed for success. I would have brought out the eagle in him. However, by quitting on his dreams and not doing all he could do to put himself in the path of success, he lost the opportunity that my mother always talked about. Mother used to say, "Opportunity lost can never be regained."

Vincent understood this. He gained a lot of corporate experience working for me at Equitable Life, then he went on to own his own printing company in Atlanta, Georgia. He later started a novelty manufacturing firm that was awarded a contract to print official T-shirts for the 1996 Summer Olympic Games. He even appeared on Bill Moyer's Journal, a national television program, just before the Olympics.

During subsequent trips to Guyana, I often saw my old buddy, John, riding that same old bicycle as I was either checking into or out of one of the various top hotels or while being driven around town by taxi. I have given him money, food and clothes. Seeing him reminds me that lost opportunities can truly never be regained.

In 1979, during my fifth year as a DSM at the Equitable agency in New York City, I requested a transfer. I wanted to get into a larger operation that offered a different leadership style. Transferring me was quite easy for the top brass to do, since I had an impeccable record. Officials at the Equitable Life home office approved my request and I joined an agency of my choice.

After a careful search, I selected the newly created Ralph Solomon agency in Lakesuccess, Long Island. Ralph was an agent who had risen to the rank of Vice President. He had an easygoing management style that made me feel very comfortable. He also had a reputation for running the agency as if it were a huge corporation. Everything about him was as smooth as silk and he had a strong commitment to making lots of money. He wore the finest threads and he was a dynamic public speaker. I learned a lot from him. One thing he would always tell his managers was this: "I am not interested in the details, only the results." He was a great leader.

I am told that he came from a very poor background, just like I did. So, I knew he shared my hunger to reach the top. Ralph, who was white, could identify with the plight of poor black people more than he would ever admit.

Shortly before I joined his agency, it had tripled in size, the result of three agencies that were merged into one. Ralph was elated to bring my five years of New York City experience to his new team. The year was 1979 and there were 13 managers in the agency at the time of the merger. He asked 11 to resign their positions. There would be one who would become his favorite. He was a veteran of about 20 years, but had never quite made the national rankings until Ralph partnered with him.

Ironically, it was while I was with this agency that I experienced my first, sour taste of bigotry. I had a much more superior record than the white favorite son, yet he was awarded many of the new hires to strengthen his team of agents. I suppose that the color of your skin really does have a lot to do with how high you can fly in corporate America.

Nevertheless, I swallowed my pride and worked hard for two more years. On one hot summer day, the Regional Vice President (R.V.P.) visited us for a State of the Agency meeting. Sitting around the egg-shaped conference room with six other

DSMs, I made my frank observations and feelings known to the R.V.P. I told him about the bigoted system that I had to tolerate. There was blatant discrimination in the hiring practices, I said. I was outnumbered at the table and clearly outranked by the R.V.P. Yet, my self-respect and my love for the insurance business led me to speak out. I wanted to be free. I wanted to spread my wings. I wanted to be the best. Thus, I spoke from my heart.

Days later, I received a very empathic and apologetic letter from the R.V.P. He offered me his full support and encouraged me to sustain my love and enthusiasm for the business and the company.

The letter was nice and I appreciated his taking the time to write it. In addition, on an intellectual level, I began to understand that the best way to fight against bigotry, which is simply groundless negative energy, is to excel and succeed at all costs—to strive to do your best with or without "their" support, endorsement or friendship. After all, success is the best reward.

Yet, on an emotional level, now that my eyes were fully opened to the discrimination and unfairness within the insurance business, I felt as if I was at a crossroads in my profession. I was despondent and wanted to quit. I had no alternative plan, no vision, but I just wanted to make a break from the frustrations of the past.

Do you ever feel that way for one reason or another? What do you do? Well, I reached out for support.

I placed a telephone call to a friendly agency manager, who was also a very nice personal friend of mine. He saved the day for me. I told Julie Goodman that I wanted to quit the business. He said to me in a very strong voice: "Victor, for God's sake, I beg you, do not quit this business. After 24 years of working in the insurance business, with all of its ups and downs, I can tell you that it is the greatest business in the world . . . *Don't quit.*"

I had never served in the army or any other armed services. I had only been a Guyana Sea Scout. With that order from Julie, however, I immediately knew what it was like to feel moved to military action. I heard what he said as if it were an order from my Sea Scout Master and I obeyed his directive. I did not quit the business, but I did change companies.

His words awakened within me something strange and wonderful. I could feel the fluttering of my spiritual faith. My spirit had wings like an eagle. Nothing could stop it from fluttering and flying. In the midst of my frustration and consternation I knew that there was an eagle within me—an eagle of greater promise and unlimited potential. This eagle, this spiritual power, would not be denied.

With my sales record in tact, my timing could not have been better to seek employment at another insurance company. I wanted my new company to have equal or superior stature and name recognition as The Equitable, which was well regarded and well known.

We have all heard the saying, "parting is hard to do." Equitable Life was my family, for better or worse. It was where I acquired the professionalism to earn a lot of money. It was where I overheard someone during a lunch break say, "I've got to get back to my desk, so I can turn some trash into cash."

What he was saying was that in the insurance business you can turn pieces of paper—telephone message pads, notes, lists and leads—into money. He was absolutely right. As insurance salesmen and saleswomen, we spent most of our time turning paper into money. I enjoyed this, yet I desired something bigger and more fulfilling than what Equitable apparently was willing to offer me. Could I find it? Would I discover a better opportunity? There was only one way to find out.

After eight years on the job, it was all over. I had helped four of my agents get promoted to DSM. I had received four National Management Citation Awards, six National Leader Honor Awards (for selling more than a million dollars worth of life insurance in one year), four President Council Citations, and I had been promoted from agent to manager. Now, it was time to say, good-bye.

As they say in the military, it was time for taps. My long, colorful and exhausting tenure ended on Friday, September 17, 1982.

I calmly removed my nameplate from my office door, locked the door and gave the keys and the remote control for the garage to the assistant manager. Then I went to my car and drove away from my private space.

Deep within I knew that this was not quitting on my dream. This transformation was necessary in order for me to find my new wings.

III

Turning Points

On September 20th, 1982 I was hired by the Allstate Insurance Company, which has a track record of excellence and community service. The company strives to live up to its motto, "You're In Good Hands with Allstate." Joining the company, I made no secret of my ethnic roots. I guess I was on a mission to beat down the walls of discrimination with professional achievement and racial pride.

Joining Allstate was a major turning point in my career and actually the beginning of many years of turning points. As an eagle swirls upward as if climbing a spiral staircase to heaven, each successive year took me higher and higher.

Not only was I experiencing turning points, the entire United States was undergoing significant changes as well. In this regard, my days as a Sea Scout served me well. Having learned Morse code in the Sea Scouts, which was founded by Sir Adam Baden Powell in England in 1907, the same year my mother was born, I found myself tapping into that skill as I sought to translate the changing American corporate code.

The corporate code was muted, yet pervasive, like Morse

code. Someone was always transmitting signals to someone else. If you didn't know how to translate the code, you didn't really know what was going on.

One of the new coded messages being sent from corporate America was that whites were afraid that the changes in the civil rights laws had liberated blacks to move into any neighborhood where they could afford to buy a home. I was one of those liberated, upwardly mobile black achievers. I moved into what was an almost all-white, middle class neighborhood in Rosedale, Queens, New York. My two-bedroom, ranch-style house on Lansing Avenue looked like the ideal businessman's house on the corner.

Whites who worked in corporate America and lived in lily white or nearly all-white neighborhoods such as this one wanted to escape the coming influx of blacks. During the decade of 1970, the flight of whites from New York City and other big cities was in high gear. Often their departure left abandoned houses, which became eyesores. This bothered me and I sought to do something about this negative phenomenon.

On one Sunday afternoon while returning home from church, I stopped off at a Martin's paint store to pick up some supplies. Also in the store was another new black resident doing just the same. As we were waiting for the cashier to ring up our bills, a conversation ensued. I said to my new neighbor, "Hey, Leonard, you see all those white folks leaving us here to take care of these nice homes. What are we going to do?"

Leonard replied, "I think that we have to do something. I don't know what."

We continued our chit chat for a few more minutes and then left the store.

I was one of the few people in the area with a gardener. One afternoon while I was washing my new Ford Mustang in front of my house, another black neighbor passed by and made mention of my well-manicured lawn. He said, "Hey, if only the other yards could look like yours, we would have a beautiful block."

Months went by, but those two brief exchanges with my neighbors stuck in my mind. Perhaps it would be beneficial to have a block association that could beautify the neighborhood, bring people together and halt the racially motivated exodus.

Just a few hundred yards down the block from me was a white couple who had lived in the neighborhood for more than a quarter of a century. I decided to ring Mr. Walls's door bell. I asked him to help me start a block association on Lansing Avenue. He was more delighted than I thought he would be.

"Surely, Mr. Babb. I'll help. Why not?"

I said, "O.K. We will start a block association." I was happy to know that we would have at least one white family participating in the new association. This would guarantee that others like him would join, too.

One of my secret personal goals was to prove that whites and blacks could live together in peace and harmony. Perhaps I believed that both sides could accept each other as decent human beings. In the old British colony where I was raised children were not taught to hate other races. Maybe we were just too busy fighting for survival. Doing anything other than putting food on the table, clothes on our backs and shelter above our heads was basically considered trivial.

The first block association meeting was held in my home. The meeting was not totally free of tension. After all, American blacks were just coming out of a very difficult period. After losing their fearless leader, Dr. Martin Luther King, Jr., and the heroic white leaders John and Bobby Kennedy, they felt betrayed by white people. They were so angry that they did not even want to talk to each other very much. They were fearful that anyone outside of their own private circles worked for the CIA or the FBI. At that first meeting there was standing room only in my finished basement.

It was a rainbow gathering, with blacks, whites and Hispanics in attendance. We quickly drew up an agenda, a mission statement and a list of goals.

The next meeting one month later was also at my home. First on the agenda was the election of officers. I was elected president of the Lansing Avenue/230th Street Block Association.

Soon afterwards, I found myself going to a police precinct for the first time in my life. As president, I was responsible for securing the permit for the organization's first block party. I wanted the party to be a huge success and I worked hard to make sure it was. I was proud to see my friend Leonard with his wife and three little children playing with the little white children in the closed off streets. All of the neighbors, their children and our invited guests were out in full force. With such positive socializing going on, we neighbors had no choice but to develop a strong bond among ourselves.

We also had now commanded the respect and attention of a whole lot of people who also wanted to and could afford to live the American Dream, including several black police officers who were retiring after 25 years of service. They were looking for shiny places to live up north, where they had found opportunity, instead of returning to the south.

The success that I was experiencing in the civic arena tasted the same and felt the same as the success I was experiencing in the corporate world. Suddenly, I realized that success in any arena is based upon the same exact principals—having a clear vision of what you desire, devising a definite plan, reaching out for support and sticking to your guns. In other words, be true to your mission and your mission will pay you your commission.

I decided that for the rest of my life I would only rub shoulders with people who wanted the same things I wanted. As you may recall, it was my mother who indoctrinated me with business. So, every since I was knee high to a puppy, I have loved business very much. Accordingly, I must be busy doing something most of the time. I dislike being at home doing nothing.

Also, I am glad that my mother did not teach me that it was morally wrong to aspire to have nice, prestigious things. Wanting to earn a lot of money and spend it on lovely things was not wrong, as long as I tithed and loved the Lord with all of my heart, she told me

Hence, I do not love money. I just like the things money can buy. I enjoy my nice neighborhood and I want to continue dressing prestigiously. And where I go to bed at night must never be slummy.

And on top of all the trappings of success, I have the spiritual foundation that Mother gave me.

In 1992 another turning point occurred. I started doing pro bono work as a Caribbean radio correspondent for WNWK, which included a stint in Guyana to report on the Queen of

England's visit. I provided reports on several Carnival celebrations as well as Expo '92. I continue to provide sports coverage for this station.

I cofounded and served as president of the Guyanese American Businessmen and Professional Association (GABPA). Later I was elected New York Chairperson of the Washington, D.C.-based Organization of Caribbean Business, Inc.

My work with the GABPA proved to be especially productive. I found myself in regular contact with other hard-working and loyal people, especially the cofounders of the organization: Carlton Guilliams, of Carl's Cosmetics; Lawrence Medas, of Medas Overseas Shipping; and Dr. Kendall Stewart, podiatrist.

Before the GABPA was founded, I had met Carlton Guilliams through an old friend and client of mine. We shared our dreams and our goals with each other and over time we gained a mutual respect for each other's vision for the future. He was just starting out in business and had a small beauty supply store on Church Avenue in Brooklyn.

As an insurance agent working in the field, I did not have to punch a clock or report for duty at any particular time. This allowed me the time to always drop by Carlton's store to check him out. He trusted me totally, hence he would leave me in the store for hours at a time so that he could run his errands and pick up supplies from the wholesaler. I observed that Carlton had the business acumen to develop a super beauty supply store, which he did.

Ultimately, we both felt that the time had come for the Guyanese business community to have our own association. We decided to solicit the opinion of Medas and Dr. Stewart, though the latter did not hail from Guyana. Still, he was a close personal friend of Carlton.

The four of us agreed to form the new association. The first meeting was held at Dr. Stewart's place, an old, two-story brownstone that he had just purchased. We nicknamed the site the "Shell," which is what we call it even to this day. **Note**: Dr. Stewart is now the leader of the Brooklyn Democratic Party.

We collectively rounded up as many Guyanese business and professional individuals as possible. On one hot and sunny Sunday evening we had 21 potential members present. I was asked to be the spokesman for this first session.

The meeting attendees were overflowing with ideas and suggestions for the new association. They were enthusiastic and hopeful that we would create something great.

Word quickly spread around town. At our next general meeting, the membership grew to 44 registered members. At this same meeting, I was elected to serve as president. Immediately after that election, a turn of events occurred that reinforced the fact that I could not place my personal feelings first when handling organizational or business affairs.

My experience with the sales manager who took exception to my bringing a female friend on the trip to upstate New York and the challenge of dealing with the racism in the corporate world had taught me how to "suck it up and hold it in." One must contain, restrain and even repress one's feelings and keep moving forward, or one might get stepped on and left behind in the hustle and bustle of life.

Several new members coming into the organization were split on the direction we should go. Half of them wanted to focus on business, while the other half wanted to get involved in the political process. The organization became fragmented for awhile. One member of the group, Roy Hastick, a free-lance printer from Grenada, saw an opening and seized the opportunity to convince several members to help him form what is now called the Caribbean American Chamber of Commerce and Industry, Inc. He credits me to this day as the cofounder of that organization, which eventually stabilized itself and grew.

Meanwhile, the GABPA became defunct. Hence, I had served as a pivot man for someone else's agenda. That sometimes happens when one dares to share his ideas publicly. That is the necessary risk you take when you attempt to make things happen. I guess you have to have a thick skin because in life you win some and you lose some.

Another turning point for me occurred when I decided to get seriously involved in politics. All of my life I shied away from politics, but as I matured, I realized that I had to pay attention to the political decisions that affected me.

I am a member of The Cathedral of Allen A.M.E. Church in Jamaica Queens, New York, where The Rev. Dr. Floyd H. Flake serves as the pastor. When Rev. Flake first ran for congressional office, I volunteered to work directly with him in his campaign. Early in his campaign, I gave Rev. Flake an idea that he used instantly.

After the death of U.S. Congressman Joseph Adabbo (D-NY), Rev. Flake was asked to run for the vacant seat. I clearly remember that it was on a hot Thursday evening in June 1986 when my good friend Nat Singleton, founder and president of the Association of Minority Enterprises of New York, came to the church with graphs and charts. He argued the case why he believed that Rev. Flake could be and should be elected to

Congress. Rev. Flake was a complete neophyte to politics. I can imagine the butterflies in his stomach as he was drafted into public office. At that very interesting, prayer-filled meeting, there was much soul-searching.

As I saw it, the most difficult decision to be made was the theme of Rev. Flake's campaign. The theme had to signify clearly what he stood for and who he was. This was a midterm election that was ordered by the governor of the state of New York. It would receive a lot of attention. His theme had to be powerful enough to create an image of confidence, competence and integrity.

By the following morning, Rev. Flake had a campaign manager in place. Within a week, Rev. Flake had accepted a theme for his campaign that one of his long-standing parishioners had given him: "Somebody Everybody Can Be Proud Of."

During the very early morning hour on the day that the Allen press in the lower auditorium of the church started running its first batch of Flake for Congress flyers, I lay in my bed reflecting on a sermon that Rev. Flake had preached exactly one year prior, entitled: "A Man of Vision." Suddenly, a spark went off within me. I jumped out of bed and rushed to the church. As I arrived, Rev. Flake was on his way out of the church. I approached him with my idea for a theme: A Man of Vision.

He anxiously replied with his usual swiftness, "Victor, that sounds good!" He paused. He smiled. Then he said firmly, "I *like* that. Go downstairs to Brother Deckie and tell him that I said, 'Stop the presses!' Change the slogan to read: 'A MAN OF VISION.'" My friend and pastor recognized that this change would be his first decisive turning point in his first run for elective office.

Later, in his five consecutive victories, Congressman Flake used the same slogan, with a slight modification: "A VISION TO DREAM." This modification reflected Rev. Flake's transcendence and maturity as a political, social and economic force for good. Experience taught him that many of us are men and women of vision, but we often lack the vision to dream the lofty dreams of freedom, power and prosperity. Such dreams are absolutely critical for those who want to achieve their highest potential.

An important dream of Rev. Flake is that one day all black people will become financially strong. He wants his people to own their homes and manage their money wisely. He recently stated to a hushed congregation in New York: "If you're renting, you're a loser."

His leadership style is often blunt, however, after this compassionate man of God chastises he always quickly follows up his criticisms with positive ideas and practical solutions for the problems facing his parishioners. He once included me in his dream to provide the people with the necessary tools to improve their money management skills.

At Rush Temple Church, also located in Jamaica, Queens, Rev. Flake was the guest preacher on a cold winter Sunday afternoon in November 1985. At that time I had been working at the Allstate Insurance Company for about three years. After the conclusion of the service, Rev. Flake and I happened to be walking towards the parking lot at the same time. We stopped to talk about his sermon, entitled, "I'm so Glad that Jesus Loves Me."

Then, he turned to me as if he had suddenly had a vision. "Victor, I would like to have a series of financial seminars at the church. Our people need spiritual and financial guidance," he said. It was a bitter cold evening. He was visibly tired from a day of giving three sermons. However, he took the time to ask me to put together a potpourri of subjects for the financial seminars.

I replied, "O.K., pastor. I would be more than happy to do it. You will hear from me. Our people do need help getting their financial houses in order. How can we get to the other side otherwise?"

This turned out to be a definite turning point in my exciting career. Coordinating and participating in the seminars would prove instrumental in my developing the ability to excel as an insurance broker and agent committed to selling millions of dollars of insurance coverage year after year.

I contacted a cadre of professional individuals to help me in this endeavor. We formed the Business and Financial Advisory Group (BFAG) and I reported back to Rev. Flake that his idea of life-changing financial seminars was certainly doable. We set February 27, 1986 as the first "Tax and Financial Planning Seminar."

Rev. Flake announced the program and pushed it from his pulpit. He was jubilant to open our first seminar himself. In his remarks he said, "I believe in Jesus Christ that He is the Truth and the Light, but we must see that Light for ourselves . . . I declare this seminar opened."

The BFAG took off like bolts of lightning in all directions. We were advising Rev. Flake's growing congregation left, right and center. Addressing the crowds that attended the seminars certainly enhanced my public speaking abilities and increased sales for me and every other group member as well: Larry Peters, CLU, of Mutual of New York; Winston Thompson, CPA; Richard Marmon-Halm, CPA; C. Theodore Wellington, attorney; Jeanna Foy, stock market specialist; the late Charles A. Smalls Sr., real estate broker, and the late Jacob Moore, V.P. at Chemical Bank. By the end of the year, we had produced more than a half dozen seminars.

    This high-powered group saw fit to elect me chairman of the board of the BFAG. Needless to say, I was honored to lead this distinguished group of skillful professionals. We expanded our seminars, hosting them at other churches and institutions around the New York City area, including Medger Evers College, Springfield Gardens Community Center, WLIB radio station, Fordham University, St. Albans Community Center, the Urban League and the Caribbean American Chamber of Commerce and Industry.

    The BFAG members gave freely of their time, knowledge and skill to people who badly needed help. I recall that one seminar attendee called me on the telephone after one of the sessions and said, "I've been married for more than 20 years, but me and my husband have never sat down to work out a budget for our family . . . Thank you for the opportunity to attend the seminar."

    Another young man called to say, "I was going to lease a car, but I'm going to buy one instead." He never understood the difference until he attended the seminar.

    A woman wrote me a note saying how much she and her husband appreciated the explanation of buying a condo as opposed to a co-op. Another young man called me to find out whether he should buy liability or comprehensive coverage for an old car that his deceased father had left for him. A teacher went to a group member's office to follow up on stock market advice. She was taught how to invest in stocks for the first time. She later shared the information with her students.

In keeping with Rev. Flake's dream, the seminars promoted a key concept, which was articulated over and over again: "Your home is your biggest bank account." We were determined to use the seminars not to only educate the people, but to stimulate them to engage in creative tax and financial planning for the future. In short, the seminars were to be used to help people make turning points in their lives.

Flash forward to 1998 and Stop the Press!

Life sure does have a strange way of presenting turning points sometimes. Just as my editor was about to send the galleys of this book to the publisher for final production, I found myself in Washington, D.C., demonstrating in front of the White House. The day was January 19, 1998, the day Americans celebrated the birthday of the late Dr. Martin Luther King, Jr.

An organization called the Guyanese and Caribbean Freedom Loving People held a march to protest against the newly elected President of Guyana, Janet Jagan, who was sworn into office on December 19, 1997 under a cloud of allegations of electoral corruption. All concerned, American-based Guyanese people, especially those living on the east coast, were invited to march for "Freedom and Democracy in Guyana, Now!"

Of course, as a concerned Guyanese, I decided to join in and to be one of the leaders of the march. Four days earlier, on January 15, 1998, more than 40,000 people had marched through the streets of Georgetown, Guyana, protesting the installation of the newly elected President. The Guyanese and Caribbean nationals vehemently opposed the appointment and the subsequent non-transparent election of Janet Jagan, an American-born woman from Chicago, Ill., and the widow of the late Dr. Cheddi Jagan, former President of Guyana.

January 19th was a significant day to hold a march, because it signified Dr. King's lasting dream of justice and equality. The march was also important for me because I have a moral obligation to stand up and protest against injustice *wherever* I find it.

This was my maiden voyage into the public arena. However, something in my heart tells me that this act of protest may prove to be one of the most important turning points in my entire life. I have always worked behind the scenes and in small forums, organizing and pushing for excellence. Yet, now I sense that politics in the years to come may somehow force me to step up to the plate.

After all, what is individual success without freedom, justice and equality for the people you love in your own home land?

No successful life is without its turning points. The best advice I can give anyone is to always be ready for change and constantly look for opportunities to make turning points. When you make the correct turn, you end up at the right destination. Just be sure to make your decisions from your heart.

IV

Success Is a Mind Game

The first three chapters of *A Golden Eagle Story* were devoted to telling you about my background and some of the milestones I have reached in life thus far. This chapter and the next two chapters are devoted to sharing with you some of the nuts and bolts of how I have built a successful career in sales.

I have found it extremely effective to see success as a mind game. Thus, I perform various mental exercises when preparing myself to make a sale. Please do not be thrown off by the term "game." This is very serious stuff.

The mind game I am referring to is actually a psychodrama guided by strong and strategic affirmations, such as those presented throughout this chapter. I use affirmations to fuel my self-confidence and sharpen my thinking, so that I can more easily channel and convince prospects to do business with me.

By being fully prepared, I will meet my future halfway.

I constantly remind myself that success in my business depends on my attitude. Having a winning attitude is a key factor in getting myself prepared to excel. My attitude has to be managed, nurtured and protected like a plant or a child. I must be able to turn on a positive frame of mind, plug into a determined spirit and activate a never-say-die attitude at the drop of a hat or the ring of a telephone. It is absolutely essential that I always be prepared to close a deal. Using this mind game, I will always be able to meet my future halfway.

My mind is searching for things to do. Thus, whatever I focus on, that is what my mind will help me to accomplish.

How do I sell millions of dollars worth of insurance in a year? I have to go after it. There is a lot of prospecting involved. A lot of night work. A lot of homework. I have to sell two medium-size policies each week and eight each month, for a total of 96 per year.

I have to approach the right people at the right time and convince them that I have what they need. **Note:** Some agents may have to sell more or fewer policies to reach the same goal, depending on their market penetration and who their customers are.

In order to perform at this level, my mind has to be climatized. I have to manipulate and control my thinking. I've got to stay focused or quickly get refocused, if I happen to lose my concentration momentarily due to the disappointments, frustrations and surprises that are bound to occur in life.

My gut will never fail me.

I get a high when I am selling, because I tune into my inner self. I let go and let my gut feeling about the prospect I am talking to guide me. Truly trusting myself and my instincts gives me a tremendous sense of freedom and confidence. As long as I observe and get to know an individual's basic personality, I can adapt to the person and speak to his or her needs and interests. I get into the heads of my prospects by asking them to tell me a little bit about themselves.

What kind of person am I talking to: liberal or conservative, calm or uptight, caring or nonchalant, intellectual or emotional? These are some of the questions going through my mind whenever I meet someone. This is part of the mind game. I fire questions at myself and my gut gives me the unspoken answer. I feel my way through each sale this way.

Every client or potential client has a different set of problems. Thus, when the phone rings, I already know that somebody has a problem. Callers are either filing a claim, or buying insurance for a new car or house. They are either trying to get something new or trying to get rid of a particular coverage that is no longer needed. I have to quickly get inside their heads and find out, "What is bothering you?" When a client comes into my office, he or she has to leave my office satisfied. A prospective client has to feel comfortable with me and informed of his or her options. These are my initial objectives.

Thus, I must serve as a counselor to people who have needs. The more intelligent a person is—notice I did not say the more educated—the better the chance of using logic and human relations skills to gain his or her confidence and close the deal.

I am here to take care of your every insurance need. I am your man. I am thee man. That's my mind-set and my mind game. When it comes to insurance, I claim my territory and I protect it.

I suggest that when you handle your business, whatever it may be, handle it as if you are the man or the woman in charge. Handle your affairs as if you are the best at what you are doing and the master of your fate. I don't care whether you are simply flipping hamburgers. Be the best darn hamburger flipper there ever was. Notice your surroundings. Take notes and take charge! Life is a game. Play to win. Flip to win!!!

Among all of the powerful affirmations and concepts that I have used to condition myself to think like a winner, the following are some of the most effective:

I have absolutely no reason not to feel confident.

I have convinced myself that selling is one of the most secure jobs in America and that the insurance industry is an anchor of the free enterprise system.

America is an insurance haven. Auto, home and life insurance are the stallions of the insurance business. These three products, which just about every adult needs, pull the entire insurance machine.

In addition, sales jobs will always be a part of our economic system. Computerization will never overtake them. A computer cannot replace a sales agent because shoppers like to hear and touch. In a car show room a car cannot sell itself; it cannot answer your questions or address your concerns. The salesperson has to be in the midst of the transaction in order to add the personal touch, the human dimension.

I can sell anything to anybody.

Why did the lemonade salesman selling for a dime sell more than the one selling for a penny? The dime lemonade salesman played a mind game, convincing himself that his lemonade was better and therefore worth more. He sold this belief to his customers and voila! He outsold the penny ante salesman. Image is everything.

I am a master at selling life insurance.

Of all of the different kinds of insurance that I sell, the most challenging is life insurance because at its core it is so intangible. It is also the product that generates the biggest first-year commission. In addition, life insurance pays residual income, thus every year a policy is renewed, I receive a royalty. I think that is simply marvelous.

While life insurance is connected to an intangible, all other types of insurance are connected to material possessions or things that you can see and touch. How can I touch someone's entire life? I can't hold someone's entire past, present and future in my hand. Thus, in order to sell life insurance, I have to create a vision of one's future that is so clear that one can see it with one's mind's eye and touch it with one's heart.

It's never too late to be a success.

Age makes me better, wiser and smarter. I welcome the aging process. It will not slow me down; it will equip me with new and better ideas, fresh concepts and innovative insights.

Bring on Grandfather Time! Have a seat, sir, and let us talk about life and all the wonders you have yet in store for me. Exercise, rest and proper dieting are all my body requires in order to continue functioning normally. My mind needs only to be filled with positive, "Yes-I-Can-Yes-I-Will" thoughts and it will stay young forever. Isn't that miraculous?

I genuinely like people and I want to help them in any way I can.

If I like people and help people and use my intelligence in dealing with people, I will never have to worry about money.

Resolving issues immediately is much better than procrastinating.

I refuse to take problems home with me. I do my best at work and move on. I have to understand the difference between what I can control and what I cannot.

My mind is like the earth. Whatever I plant in it, that's what will grow.

My mind controls what I will do. If I plant frustration, I will be frustrated. If I plant success, I will reap success because success is a mind game. If I think like a loser, I will be a loser. If I think like a winner, victory is mine.

I am a problem solver.

People need me. There is no question about it. I am in need. What I offer is in demand. I am responsible to my customers, who know they can trust me. I am always there for them. (I elaborate on this in Chapter Six: "The Sales Call." I believe you will love that chapter, because it goes into the fine details of how I have been able to sell millions of dollars of insurance year after year after year.)

The insurance business must make room for me.

As I prepare myself to reach goals, I know that the insurance business has room for people who know where they are going. Great sacrifices may be required of me in order to fulfill my dreams, for what I hope to do with ease I must first do with diligence. If I immerse myself in my work, my work will immerse me in success.

My mind is an awesome weapon. All it needs is to be pointed in the right direction.

Focusing my mind should not be hard work. It should be like a dance, like doing the Electric Slide or the Macarena. It should be as simple as playing or singing a song.

The greatest privilege in this world is to be alive. What I do between birth and death is all that counts. What I do with my life is up to me.

All I need is the right road map and, in time, I'll reach my goal. I set mini goals along the way to my big goals just to keep my spirits high. I use my road map to reach exciting financial, social and spiritual destinations.

You have in this world exactly what you dare to dream you will have. There is nothing that can stop a person with a committed heart and mind.

When I live and breathe what I believe and keep believing in my heart, though doubts may sometimes sprout within my mind, I know that I am playing the mind game very well. The trick is finding creative ways to stay there in that special space, which I call the Golden Space Within My Heart.

I am always ready to dig up the gold within me.

I am ready to dig hard. My brain is a large excavation tool. It is a strong, earth-moving, rock-chiseling mechanism similar to those mysterious machines used to shape and place the 30 thousand ton stones of the Great Pyramid.

The universe must yield to the power of the individual who totally believes in and is totally committed to reaching his or her dream. When you totally believe in yourself, you make contact with the gold glowing within you and compel things to yield to you for your purposes.

Your timing is very much in your control as well. By tuning in to who you really are and what you really want and by doing what is necessary, you will guarantee that you will surely be on time for the attainment of your life's grandest achievement.

There is a Higher Power in control.

I have nothing to worry about. I have no need to fear. Since, I have no fear, nothing I fear can ever befall me. Thus, no matter what happens, I will have no anxiety. I am definitely in good hands. Nothing can shake me from my rock of faith.

That which you fear will always befall and befuddle you.

Give no power to the false images and thoughts that lead to the anxieties and fears that often interrupt your positivity. Cast out fear by having faith in God and by using the helpful steps listed at the end of Chapter Six: "Born to Win."

I have many stars to follow.

Finding a worthy role model for success is an important facet in playing the mind game of success.

Frederick Douglass was one of the greatest figures of the 19th century. He was a leader of the Anti-Slavery Movement and a founding father of the African American protest movement. He was a huge star on the landscape of mankind.

Douglass, after escaping from slavery, educated himself and became one of the greatest speakers and thinkers of all time. He lived through one of the most turbulent and explosive eras in American history.

Douglass announced his independence from the William Lloyd Garrison wing of the Abolitionist Movement and soared to great heights as a leader of the fight against the infamous Fugitive Slave Law. It was on July 4, 1852 that Frederick

Douglass delivered his famous address on the meaning, or lack of meaning, of the Fourth of July. It was a memorable speech that was choreographed with fury and eloquence. Today, his home in Washington, D.C. is part of the National Park Service. Annually, the site attracts more than 40,000 visitors.

What success! Douglass was a descendant of stolen Africans who were trapped in slavery. After his escape, he spent two years in England, while a price was placed on his head in America. He had experienced trouble with some of his own abolitionist associates. He felt stifled by some sponsors, who were trying to control his career. Yet, he never lost sight of his goal. His freedom and his success were the end results of a mind game that he skillfully played and won. While the world called him a slave, he called himself a man—a free man, a powerful man, a supremely articulate man. And that is what he became. That is why he is one of my favorite role models.

Leaders are people who choose to lead.

I'm convinced that there's no such thing as a born leader. Great leaders are usually ordinary people who have prepared themselves for extraordinary circumstances. When I was in the Sea Scouts, the motto was: "Be Prepared." When ordinary people prepare themselves and extraordinary circumstances present themselves, these same people choose to lead because they are at the ready to take charge and succeed.

Character is like love. It cannot be bought. It can only be earned.

From my point of view, successful people manage systems, such as banks, finances, shops and computers. Highly successful people lead people.

What does it take to succeed? It takes competence. However, the single most important ingredient one needs to succeed is character. Character involves things like standards of conduct, ethics, integrity, morality and respect. Character is that intangible thing leaders possess that generates trust, love and devotion from their constituents (customers, employees, colleagues, neighbors and friends).

You never fail until you stop trying.

Getting to the top is the American way of life. Everybody wants to succeed. If the American dream can be described in one word, it's "success." That's all well and good for those who make it happen. What about those who don't?

Failure comes in many forms, too. Dealing with failure is also a mind game. If you can live your life as if you have won, though you seem to have lost, then you know how to play the game.

Some people read the newspaper sports page because it often has the most encouraging news to be found. They find stories of the winners and records of those who have excelled where the competition is keen. The sports page has sad stories, too. For every winner, there is a loser, and everyone who makes it to the top leaves someone at the bottom.

Like the best baseball hitters, let us face the fact: we lose (swing and miss, hit a foul or hit an out) more often than we win (get on base or hit a home run). Yet, just because one may lose most of the time, doesn't make one a loser.

The mother pushes her child to rank first in class. The marketing representative feels compelled to travel in the best social circles. We are all under the gun to succeed.

How do we handle it when we are not selected for that No. 1 spot at work? Overcoming failure is as simple as reminding yourself that you have won, even when you lose—if you have tried your very best. Keep improving your game and keep swinging and you're bound to get a hit.

Attorney Nelson Mandela spent 27 years in a South African jail cell for civil disobedience and for opposing the apartheid government. Some may have looked at him and seen a loser, yet it was one of the most far-reaching events in world history when on the evening of Sunday, February 11, 1990, he walked out from the darkness of confinement and into the light of freedom. He was able to rewrite history by competing in a general election. His party won and he became South Africa's first black President.

He was then able to govern his jailors and vindicate himself. If President Mandela had wasted his mind, his four children, Zinziswa, Zenani, Makaziwe and Makgatho, would not be able to say today that their father's position is a fitting symbolism in the African struggle for peace, justice and righteousness.

The world is loaded with people who are driven to succeed, but miss the bull's eye in their aim. You know some as well as I. Just to name a few: Gary Hart, who dropped out of the 1980 presidential race due to several allegations; Jesse Jackson, who has a burning desire to be President, but has not achieved that goal, yet; the United States Solicitor General who was nominated by President Reagan to be a Supreme Court Justice, but his interpretation of the law was not acceptable; Senator John Tower, who was nominated by President Bush to be Secretary of Defense, but could not make it through the same Senate that he had served.

These people remind us of the silent examples in our families, on our jobs and in our communities, our churches and even in our clubs. Their dreams are unfinished; their plans are incomplete; and their highest hopes are unrealized.

My motto for success is: "You never fail until you stop trying." If you follow my mother's way of hard work and disciplined thinking, then success is a guarantee. You cannot be a loser until you quit fighting. The romanticism of the American Dream can only happen to those who make it happen! If someone ignores the discipline that is required and quits trying, then he or she deserves to fail.

Look back in order to row forward.

My Sea Scout Master used to take his troops from Kingston in Georgetown, Guyana, to Atkinson airport, which was approximately 26 miles, in our small boat. When I was learning to row, I asked him this question: "Why do we have to look back in order to go forward?"

He replied: "Troop Leader Babb, it is automatic in this boat to look backwards in order to row forward. That is the way the boat is designed."

Success is like rowing that boat. You go forward while looking backwards. If you look at failure from a different direction, it can steer you towards your goal.

How did Columbus discover a new world? It is documented

that he set sail to discover a new passage way to India, but failed in his attempt. He failed, yet succeeded.

Raisins are actually dried up grapes, right? Was this only discovered after a farmer's entire grape crop was destroyed and he decided to see what it tasted like, hoping to salvage his investment? He tasted failure and declared it delicious.

If you put your mind to work and think hard enough, you will be able to pick out some good in every bad situation. Success is determined by your point of view. It's a mind game. You win the game when you realize that it is impossible not to find something good in every bad situation. Just keep looking.

I attribute my success (numerous Honor Rings, Chairman's Conference Awards, Life Millionaire Honors, Life Leader Honors and Management Awards, etc.) to hard work, innovations and good planning. My energy is nearly inexhaustible and my community involvement is ongoing. I attend and support career days for several New York and Long Island educational centers. I am a member of a not-for-profit group that visits a different country every year to make donations, further trade relations and work with governments to help develop countries.

I recently went to my native Guyana to present $10,000 worth of surgical supplies to the Ministry of Health. I believe that the residual from all of this activity is everlasting. To me, the world is a stage—a selling stage—on which I have to know how to put on the best performance. Every time I put together a seminar, give a speech, present a trophy or a donation, my name and my company's name are in lights.

This ongoing performance is an important ingredient in

the Victor Babb award-winning formula for service and success.

I think like a star. I act like a star. And, in Elmont, NY, I am a star!

That's my mind game—my psychodrama—and I am playing it to win.

V

The ABCs: Always Be Closing

Whether you are a novice in the sales game or quite experienced, the long and short of being very successful in this fascinating field is this: ABC. It does not mean alcohol, beer and cigarettes. It means Always Be Closing.

This is the secret to setting new sales records. You must absolutely, positively Always Be Closing.

If there is an art in sales, it is most evident during those moments when a salesperson goes for the close. When a salesperson wins a commitment from a prospect and closes a deal, it's magical, let me tell you.

However, in order to understand and master this artistic maneuver, there is no magic you must know. All you have to do is break the ABC process down into two parts.

The first part is rather simple. It entails knowledge of yourself as a sales instigator.

The second part is a bit more complex. It pertains to knowledge of your prospective buyer. Thus, the two-part process is founded on information gathering.

Let me explain:

The ABC Formula

1. Salesman, Know Yourself. First, be sure that you are fully aware of and have presented all of the benefits of your product or service to the prospect.
2. Salesman, Know Your Buyer. Be certain that you have allowed your buyer to fully express his or her needs to you. The moment you confirm this important part of the sales process is the moment of truth, for once you've accomplished that milestone, you can effectively go for the close.

Sounds too simple to believe? Well, let go of your preconceptions that a successful sale has to be difficult. Selling is simple. The key issue is how much professionalism you possess. The more product knowledge and confidence you bring to the table, the simpler it will be to close the sale and the more profitable as well. Without these important ingredients, the close is almost impossible.

Thankfully, I have lived long enough to remember well the time when a good cabbage could sell itself just by being a good head of cabbage. Nowadays it's no good just being a good cabbage. Even good cabbage has to have an advertising agent. Nothing sells itself anymore. Today it's even hard to give things away for free! Let me explain why.

Advertisers and marketing representatives rule the day. We are often taken by them. Early in the morning or late in the evening your telephone may ring with someone on the other end of the line—an advertiser or marketing rep. Quickly, with their sweet, massive verbal persuasion, some of these marketing representatives have a way of saying the correct things to you. Their words and delivery get you into the buying mood. They sort of put the monkey on your back by appealing to your inner thoughts and desires.

In order to live the American Dream, you must have a certain kind of cellular phone, they tell you. In order to feel safe in your home, you must have a certain type of alarm. In order to keep up with your neighbors, you must buy certain kinds of stocks or bonds.

In the previous chapter I stated that success is a mind game. Well, buying is a mind game also. Using the ABC principles to close a sale is definitely a mind game.

I received a call recently from my Porsche dealership. The salesperson explained to me that a new model Porsche was on the floor and that I was invited to a cocktail hour in the showroom next Friday evening to see it for myself. The sales rep further explained that I would like what I was going to see and that the price was right.

Of course, I was interested. It sounded like a good time; plus I was flattered to be invited to such an exclusive little gathering. So, I went to the reception, though I was not in the market for a new Porsche. However, the telephone call was so persuasive I went anyway. What did I have to lose, right? I was sold on the idea of being present at the gathering, which was the initial goal of the sales agent, thus the close was complete from the first moments he had me on the phone. He understood how to ABC.

What I have tried to do in all of my presentations since I joined the insurance business in 1974 is keep things simple. Simplicity is a key ingredient of the sales process. The way I sold my pots and pans in the Stabroek Market for my mother is the same way I sell today. I apply exactly the same techniques because no matter what I am selling, what I sell all depends on what my buyers can afford.

They may get a small frying pan or a big one. You should know that a small frying pan can also fry a big fish. Depending on the type of prospect I have and the circumstances under which we may have met (socially, on travel, through a friend or referral, etc.), I will use different approaches to close the sale. My colleagues have heard me ad-libbing on many occasions. What they hear is simply my tailoring my remarks to the particular person and circumstances that brought us together.

You can close a sale on almost anything without any printed material associated with it. A real estate sales person does this all the time. He or she simply shows to a qualified buyer a lovely mansion worth millions of dollars, adds her professionalism to the sales presentation and the property is sold.

I purchased my last five cars without the manufacturing blue print or the technical configurations. You bought your last car the same way. Small and large items can be closed in the most simple way. You close by degrees. You must determine whether the client has the three principal components for you to close the sale. Let me tell you what they are:

1. The client must have a need for your product or service.
2. The client must be qualified to do business with you.
3. The client and you must share mutual honesty.

Closes to Avoid

In order to Always Be Closing, you must remember that there are two typical closes that you should try to avoid, unless you are 100 percent sure of how the prospect will respond.

The first close to avoid is called the: DIRECT PROPOSITION CLOSE (DPC). It invites a very basic response: Yes or No. Use this only when you have sensed that the prospect has reached a buying decision.

The second is the: ASSUMPTIVE PROPOSITION CLOSE (APC). Use this only when you know that the buyer has reached a buying decision in your favor. For example, you can go to an APC by asking the question, "What is a good day for delivery?" Or you can say, "We take checks or credit cards only."

Winning Closes

Now that we've covered what not to do, let's have some fun talking about the correct closes to use in order to **ABC**. I recommend that you use one or more of the following closes in order get your prospect to sign on the bottom line:

BEN FRANKLIN CLOSE (BFC): Draw a vertical line down the middle of a sheet of paper, thereby creating two columns. In the left column, list all the disadvantages of your product or proposal. Ask your prospective buyer to participate. On the right side of the paper list the advantages, again getting your buyer involved in the process. Obviously, the right column (the advantages) will be much longer. Now you can go for the close.

CHOICE CLOSE (CC): You may offer the buyer a choice of items, all being suitable. For example, smiling, you can say something like this: "Would you prefer the flat paint or the oil-based one?" Or, "Would you like the 20- or 28-ounce carpet? I recommend the 20-ounce; it will do the job just fine, and, of course, cost less."

MINOR OBJECTIONS CLOSE (MOC): Listen carefully to the minor objections from the buyer. Respond to them item by item as though they were major, sale-stopping issues. I guarantee you that the customer will compliment you on being a good listener.

SUMMARY BENEFITS CLOSE (SBC): Some customers do not expect to be told all of the features of your product. They may not be interested in all of them, either. In this case close by summarizing the benefits. Don't overwhelm your customers with all of the goodies. Just remind them that this is exactly what they are looking for.

LOSS OF BENEFIT CLOSE (LBC): This approach is exactly what it says. "You, (Mr. or Ms. Prospect) will lose . . . (this or that benefit), if you do not act now. By acting today, you will be guaranteed a special rate (or discount). So, why not take advantage of our special offer before it runs out?" Let me give you another example of the LBC. Recently, one of my clients asked me to look into the best price and finance rates for a new car. After calling up a few dealerships, I decided to go in to see one of them. Sure enough, the salesman was able to convince me that that very day was the last day for a special discounted finance rate from a particular bank. He said, it was late in the day, but he believed that he could still get it for me. Whether what he was saying was true or not—and I sincerely believe he was being truthful—the rate was the best I had seen. The salesman was able to close that deal the same evening.

TESTIMONIAL LETTERS CLOSE (TLC): This is quite different from name dropping. If you have some legitimate famous or well-known clients in your data base, you can use them, but be careful because some may get offended. Use your gut feelings as to when to use these letters. When in doubt, you can tell a prospect that people in his or her neighborhood are already happy customers of yours. This is just as effective.

In order to ABC, you must always be confident. If you are not confident with your product or your presentation, it will manifest itself to the client via your closing statements. When closing, be sure to ask leading questions that will generate immediate action. Stay away from questions such as "I'm sure everything is clear to you? Or, Is there anything else you'd like to know?" Also, avoid saying, "Do you understand everything I've said?" A positive closing question would be: "You are qualified! So, why don't we complete some details?"

By using this proactive strategy, you reinforce the need to take action now. Don't raise doubts about the prospect's willingness to act now. Go for the close as if the prospect really wants what you are selling and is simply waiting for you to say the right words, but don't be too hasty. Pace yourself, trust yourself and feel your way through it.

Smooth Moves at Closing

BRIDGING THE GAP: In some cases your timing may be way off. This happens to the best salesman in the world, especially if he is a bit absentminded. Sometimes a salesman's thoughts may drift to the previous sale or the future sale. If the customer objects to your early close, then you will have to apologize. You can say, "Oh, all I'm trying to say is that this product meets your needs, doesn't it?" Or better yet, you can say, "I realize that you may still have a question or two for me." Then, move smoothly to the final close by summarizing the benefits again. Get your prospect to accept some minor agreements. Obviously, your prospective client is not in too much of a hurry. Again, be careful not to go too fast for the prospect, for if you miss the second trial close, you will be sorry.

THE SILENT RULE: Keep quiet once you have made your closing statements. It is always courteous to wait for a response. The customer will notice whether you respect his or her thoughts. How many times have we heard that silence is golden? I've heard it since I was a child and more than likely so have you. This rule works well in sales. It's amazing, but you can actually keep the pressure on with the right amount of silence. It also gives you the advantage of checking the customer's verbal, nonverbal, conscious and subconscious attitudes toward your product. The customer knows full well that your respectful silence is designed to generate an answer.

RELATIONSHIP BUILDING: The final moments are to build and cement a relationship, whether the close was successful or not. This is a very essential point. Keep your customer engaged in lighthearted conversation while you are completing the order. At this point silence is not golden. It can create a question from out of left field. So, at this point in the transaction do not go over the benefits of the product. Focus instead on relationship building.

Also remember that customers are inhibited by paper work

and computers. If you are using a paper application, have it out already. If you are using a computer, have it on when the customer arrives.

Use a good writing pen and keep a clean, clear desk. No clutter. (Clutter will cost you.)

While you are preparing the paper work, engage your customer in conversation about some kind of financial advice you can offer. Keep your customer talking by discussing with him or her these 10 money principles:

1. Make joint financial decisions with your spouse.
2. Save at least 10 percent of your monthly income in a short-term emergency fund. One way to save is to do things that are pleasurable, but don't cost a lot of money.
3. Don't procrastinate about establishing financial goals.
4. Properly insure your life, health, home and auto. Review and perhaps replace any ordinary life insurance policy that is more than five years old. It's probably obsolete. Always seek qualified help.
5. Maintain a good credit rating by paying your bills, not over spending and avoiding most credit cards. Postpone buying expensive cars, lavish clothes, etc. during early years of marriage.
6. Own rather than rent housing for tax benefits.
7. For your child's college education consider putting some funds in an insurance policy or purchasing Series EE U.S. Savings Bonds, which allow you to defer tax on the interest until the child is fourteen. Also, consider buying tax-exempt municipal bonds.

8. You can postpone setting up an Individual Retirement Account (IRA) until you are in your 40s. However, if self-employed, you must have an IRA.
9. For long-range financial growth, invest in equities (mutual funds, stocks, bonds, limited partnership real estate deals, etc.), but purchase individual stocks only with the help of a professional money manager.
10. If your annual income is more than $75,000 you should consult a professional financial planner.

Other principles of relationship building are as follows:

After the paper work is ready to be signed, carefully obtain the customer's signature. To ask for someone's signature has an unpleasant connotation. Depending on the situation or the prospect, you may or may not have a conversation at this juncture. There are many different ways to ask for a signature. The universal one is: "Mr. Customer, may I have your John Hancock?" Or "Ms. Customer, can you initial here for me?" Another common request is: "Mr. Customer, please O.K. this order on this line." Or "Ms. Customer, you can sign here in full." Just to name a few.

Think On Your Feet

The challenge of Always Be Closing is one of the greatest tasks anyone can face because it requires you to think on your feet. This trait is often described as flamboyance. Interestingly, customers like to deal with these kind of people. I believe customers can feel when they are being catered to. So, remember that the powerful selling phrase that you used on one prospect won't necessarily work on others. You have got to come up with new phrases and dialogs all of the time. In this way Always Be Closing is similar to always be on your toes.

In order to pick up good information and catchy phrases, read books and magazines and watch popular television programs.

For instance, I picked this one up some time ago: "We do it the old fashion way. We earn it." To be powerful and world class you must have and use fresh material all of the time. Like the comedian, you must think of fresh material and new lines constantly. The comedian is always going for the punch line. When he's working, everything he says and does is designed to get you to laugh. As a salesman, everything you do is designed to close the sale. From the moment you meet someone, you have got to be focused on closing the sale. This doesn't mean you have to go for the hard sell. It means you have to be intelligent, skillful and personable.

Never forget that each customer, each call, each presentation and each closing is unique and requires creativity, planning and a polished performance.

Rehearse, Rehearse, Rehearse

Rehearse your approaches in your mind or with a colleague. Repeat and visualize what you are going to say. How firmly should you state your words? How fast or slow should you talk? We're all different. Find your best communication style by practicing and asking for critiques. Tape record yourself and critique yourself. Habitually practice your skills. Try to predict objections to your product and prepare appropriate responses. Relax and enjoy this growing process, which I call getting great in the game.

Don't be embarrassed or too shy to practice over and over. Remember, presidential candidates practice their debates. Championship boxers and tennis players and golfers and other top athletes practice as if practicing is their religion. They rehearse their moves and deliveries as if their lives, not just their livelihoods, depend on it. Sales people should be no different. If you are really serious about being No. 1, try it.

Show Yourself the Money

Your closing ratio is totally dependent upon your own efforts. The process of becoming as financially independent as one desires is an integral thread that runs through the core of the American Dream. Thus, it is normal to seek wealth in America. When you close a sale, think of how closer you will be to getting there. America needs you to become rich, for she cannot afford to do without her wealthy people.

Wealthy folk create opportunities for all Americans to become employed and productive and to live well. Remember the Golden Rule when you are asking your buyer to sign on the dotted line: "Do unto others as you would have others do unto you." Backing up this note, remember the 10 P's. (The successful journalist never forgets the five W's and the H—who, what, when, where, why and how—and the successful salesman or saleswoman never forgets the 10 P's.) The 10 P's are easy to remember because they form a complete sentence: Pride, Patience, Purpose, Persistence, Perspective and Proper Planning Prevent Poor Performances.

Attitude Adjustment

In the sales business, it is critical to keep an upbeat attitude. So, what happens on those days when you just don't feel so upbeat? What can you do to break through the blahs when you have to perform? In order to Always Be Closing, you need a handful of proven ways to put some spark into your morale because it will be difficult to close, if you feel down. Here are my six rules for attitude adjustment:

1. Your outlook will improve, if you have something specific to strive towards. For instance, say to yourself as you go for the close: "This is for the baby." Or, "This is for the new house I am going to buy." Or, "This is going to help me take that vacation I need." So, select a goal and be determined about it.
2. Learn more about your career, your company and interpersonal relations. Knowledge gives you more things to talk about and will improve your performance.
3. Talk to someone who usually speaks in positive terms. Positive behavior is contagious. Let it rub off on you.
4. Do not put off projects that should be accomplished today. Procrastination is the thief of time. Instant gratification helps to improve one's outlook. Tackle lingering chores. This will give you a sense of accomplishment that will spill over into your sales presentations.
5. Commit to improving yourself regularly and consistently. Maintain the thought that you will be better off tomorrow than you are today. Concentrate on

improving your memory. Buy books on this subject. Your voice and posture may need improving a bit. Work on these things and you'll feel better.
6. Lastly, but certainly not least, act enthusiastically; sit or stand with proper posture and walk with purpose, pride and dignity. Hold your head up high, even if you are simply going to the store to buy a hot dog or a cup of tea.

The Sole Secret of Success

The sole secret of success is this: more is always within you. If you want to do something, you have to make it happen. Sometimes we hold back due to fear of failure or fear of succeeding. Believe in yourself. Believe that you can do more and you will. To Always Be Closing you must always be dreaming and striving for your goals. Don't wait for later. Do it now!

Anything is possible, if you want it badly enough and are willing to pay the price to close the sale. It demands discipline.

Being creatures of habit, when we have too many bad habits we doom ourselves to failure and frustration. We put ourselves out of the game. Bad habits get you off of the path of success that you have worked so hard to reach. Especially avoid these bad habits: socializing in the workplace with the wrong people; excessive coffee and cigarette breaks; procrastinating about calling for appointments; quitting too early after the customer says, "No;" avoiding activity that you do not like.

Now for the good habits: selective socializing; spending dollars to make dollars; always looking for leads; soliciting the advice of professional advisors, such as CPAs, attorneys, etc.; getting into the habit of reading everything you can get your hands on, if it pertains to your business; constantly upgrading your clientele.

If you truly want to sharpen your skills at closing, remember to be a "pro" by looking like a pro. Dress the part. Polish your image. Build a good reputation in and out of the office. Know what are the "Golden Hours" for your line of business. Make a list of the best business customers you deal with and go and see them personally.

It takes the same time to find someone earning $25,000 a year as it does to find someone earning $100,000, depending on where you are looking. In presenting your product, remember the K.I.S.S. principle: "Keep It Simple and Sincere." Always remember that people buy when they understand. Don't play the role of "professor." It is a turn off.

As you wrap up your sales presentation, start to close the minute you see the opening. Fight for the sale like your life depends on it. Only you know what you want in life. Do whatever it takes to make it happen (without exceeding moral and legal limits, of course).

In conclusion, I would like to share with you my:

12 Commandments for Closing the Sale

1. Thou shalt rehearse closing techniques.
2. Thou shalt have confidence; you've got to, got to, got to believe.
3. Thou shalt either specialize or generalize.
4. Thou shalt qualify your prospect.

5. Thou shalt get involved in your community.
6. Thou shalt be a professional.
7. Thou shalt sell what the customer wants for today and tomorrow.
8. Thou shalt always give a choice.
9. Thou shalt set goals.
10. Thou shalt have a Positive Mental Attitude (PMA).
11. Thou shalt have total commitment.
12. Thou shalt improve thyself.

Man's only limitation, basically, lies in his development and the use of his imagination (planning). No individual has sufficient experience, education, native ability and knowledge to ensure the accumulation of great fortune, without good planning, which usually entails the cooperation of other people. Many people go through life in misery and poverty because they lack a sound plan of action.

Many people who have accumulated fortunes did so not because of their superior minds, but because of their superior plans. No man is ever whipped until he quits in his own mind. Anyone in the world can turn defeat into victory through a new plan—especially you.

If you commit yourself to Always Be Closing and the principles and ideals underlying this concept, you cannot fail. I guarantee it!

VI

The Sales Call

What is a sales call?

A sales call is created every time someone is faced with a purchase decision. The average person wants to feel comfortable and needs to be convinced as to what he or she should do. Thus, a sales call is simply an opportunity for a salesman to gain the trust of a person and to convince that person to do something.

My basic sales call protocol consists of a collection of tested and proven strategies for gaining the trust of the prospect. I will demonstrate my technique shortly, but first I would like to emphasize a point I made in earlier chapters of this book. In order to make a sales call successful, I have to be knowledgeable of my product, my prospect and myself. The most important thing to know about myself is that I am a special person, particularly because it takes a special person to sell life insurance. Why? Because life insurance is in a league all by itself. As I stated in an earlier chapter of this book, life insurance is connected to an intangible.

Selling life insurance is different than selling cars, computers, homes or any other product that you can see, touch and feel. When I sell a life insurance policy, I am selling a vision, a dream and a sense of security. I protect you when you are not here anymore to protect yourself. I protect your family and your home and the future of your children. I even protect your good name and your credit by making sure that all of your bills are paid. I keep your financial house in order when you are not here to do it for yourself. I empower you to educate and care for your children from the grave. When you are not breathing any longer, your love and wisdom will continue to keep your offspring warm and secure—through your life insurance policy.

A car cannot do that. A house, if the mortgage goes unpaid, cannot do that. A computer definitely cannot do that. Life insurance *can* do that.

At the risk of being redundant, let me say this: People who know that they are special and that life insurance is special and that every prospective policy holder is special are ready to make this special kind of sales call.

Now, isn't that special?

Would you like to know what successful insurance sales agents are thinking? They are constantly thinking about positive realities—that they are alive and well, and that they belong to a profession that allows more freedom than most. They are thinking that their lives are worth living to the fullest and that if they direct their energies to serving their customers fully, they will experience much more happiness than the average person.

Finally, they are thinking that it is their privilege and pleasure to be of infinite service to the community.

Knowing that I am selling people something that is going to help improve their lives produces a tremendous high in me.

No artificial stimulant can do this. When I know my job has been done well, as though no other person could do it any better, the satisfaction is indescribable. When someone wants to spread the word for me, that takes me to yet another level. Hearing the word "referral," I envision my bank account growing larger. Therefore, I get excited whenever a client of mine says, "I have a friend, can you help him?"

With that primer, you are now ready to go with me on a sales call.

Note: I will use as an example a fictitious character, a composite of many of my present clients. I will call her Mrs. Love. My objective today is to sell her a life insurance policy. She is already an automobile and home insurance client of mine, as are most of my life insurance prospects. I have decided to draw her name today at random.

With my millionaire attitude in full effect, I call her at home after work.

Setting the Appointment

"Hello, Mrs. Love, my name is Victor Babb, your Allstate insurance agent. How are you doing this evening?"

She responds, "I'm fine, and you?"

"Fantastic, Mrs. Love, thank you for asking." **Note**: it is essential to dialogue before getting into asking for the appointment. Try something lighthearted such as talking about the weather, for example.

"I was going through my records and I noticed that you recently got married and that you and your husband have just bought a house together. I am calling to congratulate you and to ascertain whether you and Mr. Love might be interested in protecting your family's new investment for the long term. After another brief exchange, I ask for an appointment with her and her husband, giving a choice between Tuesday and Thursday evening.

She responds, "Thursday."

"Would 7:00 p.m. be O.K. or would 8:00 be better?"

She says, "8:00 would be fine."

Creating the Right Environment

Once I get into the home, I immediately ask for either a desk or a table (dining room or kitchen) where I can place my documents, discuss the proposals with them and make my winning presentation. I've got to create the right environment to be effective.

Introducing and Selling Myself

Before discussing business, I take a few minutes for casual conversation, such as complementing the prospects on their new home and decor. Since most people do not like to be sold, this is intended to create a more personal and relaxed atmosphere and take the edge off of what might be a tense situation. **Note:** Remember, Always Be Closing!

It is now important to establish the credentials of the company and the salesperson. This information serves to instill respect in my prospects. It lets them know that I am serious about my job. **Note:** If I lacked experience, I would stress my commitment to become the best in the business.

"Mr. and Mrs. Love, my company has been in business for over 65 years and is one of the most respected insurance companies in the industry," I say. "I personally have been in the insurance business for 24 years and have developed a superior track record of servicing my clients. I also offer you 24-hour-a-day service. In addition, my licensed and trained office staff offers ongoing support to meet all of your insurance needs. As one of Allstate's top agents, I understand what it means to help to protect people like yourselves. I would like to share two proposals with both of you that will lay out the details of a life insurance plan to make sure that no matter what may happen in the future, your home will always be paid for. Does that sound like something that would interest you?"

Both prospects nod, yes.

The Presentation

Note: I always expect objections and look for ways to work around them.

Mr. Love: "What you are saying is interesting, but we already have insurance on our jobs."

Salesman: "That's fine, however, what if the job leaves you or you leave the job?"

Mrs. Love: "I like my job and I have job security."

Mr. Love: "So do I."

Note: I do not get caught up in a long debate about the prospects' jobs. Instead, I stay focused on moving towards the close. "Now that you have a new mortgage to pay, shouldn't you consider additional insurance?" I respond. "As I said, I brought two proposals with me tonight that I would like to briefly review with you to see how each would fulfill your current needs."

I now take the time to review the proposals and answer additional questions or objections.

The Close

Once you feel comfortable that you have answered all of their questions, ask a specific closing question that does not require a yes or no answer. Use an either/or question, such as: "Which proposal do you feel suits your needs better, Plan A or Plan B?"

Now, I do not say another word. I wait until the prospects respond.

Mr. Love: "The plan for $1,200 per year will do the job."

I confirm the response by asking for their Social Security Numbers and other personal data.

My mother gave me an important piece of advice a long time ago: "It's not what you say, but it's *how* you say it that matters." Therefore, as I wrap up a sales call, I change my sitting position, projecting a very relaxed and sincere aura. I look my new customer in the eye and say with confidence and conviction, but not with excitement, a phrase such as, "I congratulate you for making this important decision for you and your family." I speak slowly, softly, clearly and precisely to convince the prospect that I am sure of myself and that they have just made a decision that is in the best interest of the family. This final verbal handshake and pat on the back helps to keep customers from changing their minds later, after I have left.

Important Sales Qualities

To be successful in sales, you need to be skilled. This requires ongoing training and experience. You need to be able to recognize the prospect's signals, both verbal and nonverbal, positive and negative. You need to look and act like a professional—in your attitude, speech and attire. You can never be too neat; so, keep your shoes shined, nails groomed, etc. It is the whole package that the customer is looking at!

When I first started in the insurance business, I worked day and night, calling on the phone, prospecting, and setting up appointments. Once you acquire longevity in this industry, people respect you and your closing ratio goes up. You start at the bottom on smaller cases and then start to advance to larger policies. After awhile, you have the clientele and confidence to sell million dollar policies. No one starts out selling million dollar policies. Your prospects want to know that you have proven yourself as a career professional insurance agent.

How To Deal With Difficult Prospects

I love a challenging prospect. In fact, the more challenging the prospect, the more confidence I generate. I feel comfortable responding to objections with affirmative answers. I enjoy explaining to intelligent people the meaning of insurance. The following is an example of how I would handle a difficult prospect.

The prospect, Mrs. Tomlin, is very skeptical about buying life insurance. She has invited me to her office because she likes me and wants to hear more, but she is not ready to commit.

"Thank you for taking the time to see me, Mrs. Tomlin," I say. "As you know, I would like to discuss your insurance needs. May I have your date of birth, please?"

Mrs. Tomlin: "May 3, 1942."

"What type of insurance would you like?"

"Well, I don't know. To be truthful, I really feel that insurance is just a 'rip off!'"

"Mrs. Tomlin, if insurance was a rip off, no insurance agent would be in business."

Mrs. Tomlin: "Well, I don't know. Maybe the politicians are in cahoots with the insurance bosses and they turn a blind eye to all the rip offs going on in the industry."

"In the past five years I have delivered three death claims to families who needed it because the breadwinner had died. Those families did not consider it a rip off when I handed them checks for $100,000 or more. I had one client who, unfortunately, was shot dead during a robbery. I took the money to his family members. They felt relieved to know that he had thought enough of them to look after their needs in case of an emergency. No rip off there, wouldn't you agree?"

Mrs. Tomlin: "You know that makes sense, but I have investments. I've got equity in commercial properties and I own stock. When I die, all of that will go to my heirs. So, why would I need life insurance?"

"Since you own property and stocks, first of all, I congratulate you. This means that you are worth a lot of money right now. But, have you ever considered insuring your future earning power? Let me show you a plan that will take care of that if you become sick or disabled. The investment earnings that you hope to gain in the future are great, I am sure, however, a life insurance policy will *guarantee* that you will have funds in the future, for in life, as quiet as it's kept, you either die too soon or live too long. In either case, a life insurance policy will benefit you either directly or indirectly.

"If you die early, life insurance is the only thing that will produce guaranteed cash for your heirs. This is a good reason to get a policy now. And if you live very long, it is better to get a policy now, as well, so that you can take the money out and enjoy it in your old age.

"I will show you how to use our retirement pension and savings plan. It's a nest egg that everyone should have for his or her future because with life insurance, you can't lose. Your heirs will get paid if you die before age 65 and if you live beyond 65, we will pay you when your policy matures. It is your right as an individual to have such a powerful tool of financial protection."

Note: Mrs. Tomlin is simply looking at me now. Finally, she says the only thing she possibly could say:

Mrs. Tomlin: "Yes, Mr. Babb, you are absolutely right."

"Thank you, I appreciate your acknowledging the logic of this concept . . . Now, what is your Social Security Number, Mrs. Tomlin and who is your beneficiary?"

Note: I am now moving in for the close because she agreed with me. Never lose sight of a closing opportunity!

"Life insurance has its place," I say. "When you die, your bills do not die with you. Someone else has to pay for them when you are gone. The beauty of life insurance is this: when you die you can still take good care of your family and even educate your children from the grave. Imagine that! In addition, insurance allows you to buy money at today's discounted rates.

For example, the older you get, the more an insurance policy will cost you, especially if you are in poor health."

Mrs. Tomlin:: "I guess what you are saying is that the proper way of looking at life insurance is as protection, as a rock solid investment?"

"You've got it! Life insurance is one of the best investments you'll ever make."

Note: She has given me a clear signal that she has sold herself and that I have convinced her that life insurance is certainly not a rip off, but an important investment for her future. Her transformation from skeptic to believer underscores the reason that it is important to get this important message to every life insurance prospect: *insurance is all around us.* Our homes are protected; our cars are protected; our expensive jewelry is protected; our businesses are protected. But is your life protected? Are those material possessions more important than your life? Material possessions can be replaced, but not your life!

The Power of the Proposal

I have been using proposals as sales tools for 24 years. I am now a master of the art of selling with a proposal. My first sales manager, Ted, would always remind me to prepare proposals for all of my sales calls. Back then, in the early 1970s, we did not have computers at our fingertips. Proposals were ordered from the home office. The waiting period was two-to-three days. Nevertheless, I was patient to wait for them to arrive in the mail. I knew that once the proposals arrived, I would be able to turn paper into money!

In today's marketplace we have come a long way, with desktop computers and small, handy printers. As a result, the insurance agent can now generate a printed proposal on top of the kitchen table, right in front of the prospect's eyes. Amazing!

Let's take a good look at how to prepare a proposal before going on a sales call.

A proposal is nothing less than a conduit between the sales agent and the customer. It is a person-to-person selling mechanism. It is also a visible, tangible thing that creates a point of sale wherever it is presented. A spotty, creased or blemished proposal can jeopardize your selling effort.

Stay away from brochures at all times when presenting a proposal, because they can distract the client from the proposal. Use highlighters to point out the important features in the proposal and that includes your prospect's name. The proposal empowers you to immediately take control of the sales call, especially if you arrive on time for the appointment.

Good Reasons to Use a Proposal

1. A proposal shows that you are adequately prepared for your sales call.
2. A proposal gets the client thinking about the numbers.
3. A proposal can be initialed by the client and kept on file.
4. A proposal decreases the customer's wavering mind and unanticipated demands.
5. In today's high tech society, a proposal gives you the image of a polished pro.

6. The client is making a major buying decision and you want him or her to feel good about it. A proposal can help because it is a hard and fast document containing real numbers. It commands respect.
7. The customer will see what you are proposing because it is all on paper.
8. A proposal will communicate exactly what you are selling and present all of the financial rewards that the customer will receive.
9. A clearly defined proposal sets your product a part from the competition.
10. A proposal defuses any criticism from the prospect's spouse or company insurance rep regarding whether the prospect has been presented with what is needed to make a complete comparison of benefits and services.

Remember that it is in both your interest and your potential client's interest to nail down the appropriate proposal. In particular, you benefit because the proposal decreases the chances of your being accused of making innocuous promises and confusing terms. A proposal should always be an original copy and hand delivered by you because you may not be present when the final decision is made by the prospect. If the proposal is not prepared with the utmost of care, it will weaken your chances of getting the prospect to sign it. One mistake to avoid is to be so confident about your proposal that you will review it for the first time in the presence of the client.

I always like to deliver my proposals in person. It gives me the added advantage of witnessing my client's reaction. If I must send a proposal by mail, I send it "Special Delivery" for a touch of class.

It may be necessary for your manager to approve your proposal. This is a very good idea. It demonstrates a high degree of commitment by the company. A proposal signed by a senior person in your organization shows that a second opinion was involved. It's the old two against one scenario. The odds will be in your favor. The manager's signature also underscores that your proposal has integrity.

My many years of experience have proven to me that the length of a proposal depends on the type of client with whom I am dealing. In addition, I will often reinforce my proposal with a cover letter, particularly if I am dealing with a customer who is an executive.

During the early stages of my insurance career, Ted told me that I would make or lose a sale during the first two minutes. Therefore, I always want to be sure that my cover letter and proposal will hit home during the first two minutes of the prospect's time. If I write a cover letter, I must be certain that it has at least three effective, low-key paragraphs.

The first paragraph refers to the last conversation between me and the prospect and mentions that a proposal is enclosed. The second paragraph reiterates the kind of service that the prospect can expect from me and announces everything else that I am prepared to do for the customer. It also briefly explains why the enclosed proposal fits his or her needs. The final paragraph deals with the financial condition of my company. For instance, it will tell the customer the impressive ratings of the company. Finally, this last paragraph asks the prospect for his or her business.

Do you see the simple logic and the pure psychology at work here? Hopefully, it is clear that in the final analysis the real purpose of a cover letter is to sell me and my company. It is designed to convince the prospect that we are serious, we are good at what we do and we really want his or her business.

Prospecting and Referrals

A proposal is no good if no one wants to see it. This is where prospecting comes in. Regardless of the type of sales business that you are in, prospecting will always be involved and referrals will always be necessary. You must find the person with the problem that you can solve.

I jot down on a list the names of prospects and referrals. On a continual basis, I decide in my mind what I think they should buy. Then I print some proposals and begin calling the people on my list. Before you know it I have a few scheduled appointments.

Let me share two different incidents that occurred because I had followed up with names that were on my list: I met a man at a birthday party. He showed interest in purchasing a life insurance policy, specifically for his family. When I returned to my office, I placed his name on my "hot" prospect list. Soon after, I called to arrange an appointment. Once I was able to talk to him personally, I convinced him to take out a policy for himself as well as his family. Ironically, just a few weeks after I wrote both policies he died.

The second example of the importance of keeping a prospect list occurred in connection with a gentleman who was a very dear friend of mine for many years. I had watched him go from business to business, unsuccessfully, and I never believed that one day he would turn out to be an important client of mine. His name kept going from list to list because he continued to procrastinate about making a buying decision. Even after he got married and had two children, I still could not nail him down. One day this friend invited me to his home for lunch. During our conversation, he casually asked me how much life insurance I thought he needed.

I replied, "About $100,000."

He looked me straight in the eye and said, "How about $1,000,000?"

I almost fell off my chair, but I calmly responded, "How is your health?"

He said, "Great!"

I said, "You got it!"

Another anecdote that I will share is about a client, a retired New York City Transit worker, who was on my list. Three years after I sold him a $100,000 policy and one year after he retired, he died, and I delivered the claim check to his wife. Because of a simple list and a follow up sales call his family ended up with money, instead of only burying a husband and father and mourning his loss.

Because of these simple success stories, where timing turned out to be perfect under different circumstances, I feel uncomfortable when I'm sitting in my office and not in the "field" meeting with prospects. To overcome this anxious feeling, I get on the phone and call anyone on my list. I am totally convinced that if I do nothing, nothing will happen. In fact, I have a sign hanging in my office that reads "You Never Fail Until You Stop Trying."

Do you know how simple it is to set up a sales call? All I need is a telephone, a post card or a pre-approach letter. It is that simple! These outreach tools alert prospects that you will be contacting them soon. When I think that the prospect does not want to see me or is too busy to schedule an appointment, I do not call. Instead, I will send a letter. We are now living with voice mail and, lo and behold, I have had to change my strategy. When I leave a voice mail message, I make the best possible use of it. I script the exact words needed to incite interest and generate an appointment. I say what I plan to say and do not repeat it. I never anticipate any barriers, for if I look for them, I will surely find them. I must keep a positive attitude and control what influences my thinking. This is especially true now that I am the boss, running my own agency with my name on the bold, blue and white shingle.

Honesty Sells

This business has taught me to be frank and open. I have never been asked to leave an appointment for telling the truth. Honesty is communicated in various ways. When making a sales call, I am sure that my business card is neat and clean. I treat it like my passport to get in the door. When I return to the office, I follow up with a thank you letter, especially when I am dealing with a business account.

Get Emotional

I have found that often during sales calls, logic is not always enough to persuade my prospects. I have to get evangelical when making a sales presentation. I have to appeal to their hearts and not their brains. They must feel the electricity in me. They must sense my sincerity. They must participate in the excitement of the sale. I must connect with them, so that on a gut level I can sense when they are ready to buy. I must actually measure the enthusiasm or doubt in them.

Is this magic? No, it's science—the science of the sale. Emotion transforms dull interviews into exciting ones and helps me to connect with prospects. Like a doctor in the examining room, I feel their pulse and their visceral reaction to what I am saying. I sense their frame of mind. Like a surgeon in the operating room, I transplant doubt and the urge to object with faith and the urge to say, "Yes!"

My prospects must believe in me. My confidence must radiate. When I am on a sales call, I get personal while I present the proposal.

Again, it's really not the proposal I am selling; it's me and the company I represent. It is like proposing marriage; it isn't the ring, it's the man.

Think about it, if a bum offers an expensive ring to a lovely lady, she will not marry him just for that alone! She wants a complete package. So do my customers.

Lifting Myself Up to the Sales Challenge

During any sales call I always talk to myself, but never out loud. The top question is, "Am I at the level of selling expertise for this particular prospect?" The answer to myself is always an emphatic, "Yes!"

Next, "Will I have more than one opportunity to close this

sale today?" The answer is, "No, this is a one-shot deal. If I do not close this sale today, I probably will never be given a second chance. Therefore, I must give my very best performance. <u>Opportunities lost can never be regained.</u>"

As I stated earlier, the more challenging the prospect, the better. For the higher up I reach to make the sale, the stronger and more confident I will be and the more effective my presentation will be. While I am super sure of myself today, my confidence did not grow over night. I have pinpointed five distinct selling phases that over the years have lifted me up to the point where I can now meet any selling challenge:

1. The Year of Uncertainty
2. The Breakthrough Years
3. The Grooming Professional Years
4. The Sales Management Seasoning Years
5. The Independent Victor Babb Agency Development Years

During my Year of Uncertainty I was anxious. I was always in a hurry to learn everything I could about selling insurance. My mother had taught me the basics of selling, but I needed expertise in this, my chosen field of specialization. I can remember once taking out my clients' garbage at the end of the sale. I was so excited I would have done almost anything to show my appreciation. During this period I always felt as if I needed to have a sales manager inspect and approve my work.

However, by June 1, 1975 it was clear to me that I had stepped into the Breakthrough Years. My personal sales call success ratio was so high that I was promoted to manager. In that same year I was selected Manager of the Year. In my new role as manager my job was to show the new trainees how to make sales calls. I knew they were nervous. Heck, I was nervous myself because in some ways I was both a trainee agent and a rookie manager. I was paying the price of success, having been shoved into a position of greater responsibility. Going out with my trainees on sales calls was always a fantastic thing for me to do during my Breakthrough Years.

The Grooming Professional Years began with a visit to the tailor. My new, custom-made suit signaled that I had arrived as a professional. **Note:** Pumping up, yet controlling your ego is not something to be taken for granted.

Also as part of my Grooming Professional Years, my strength as a manager was increased. At the beginning of this period, I only knew 50 percent of how selling really works, notwithstanding the years of training and experience I had racked up. As a rookie manager I needed to spend time with senior management in order to gain in-depth experience and enhance my ability to see the big picture and how the system truly works.

Rubbing shoulders with successful managers is what was needed to solicit off-the-cuff answers regarding new strategies for making sales calls. This alone helped me to reach a higher level of understanding. During these years I learned that keeping an open mind is not only common sense, it is critical.

Five years later, during my Sales Management Seasoning Years, I felt a high level of selling competency. It was then that I knew how to sell and how to close even the most difficult sales calls. I developed the correct timing for working the customer.

I became totally in control of my interviews. The questions I asked were more specific. I knew every possible set of answers before the customer opened his or her mouth. I listened more and presented exactly what was needed to convince anyone with a logical mind that there really were no justified objections to what I was offering. Suddenly, there were no more wasted proposals.

I gained a better understanding of my tactical skills. I became more aware of my strategic planning skills. During these years I relied on the buyer throughout my sales calls and no one else. I stopped concentrating on price and instead focused my attention on benefits and services. Looking to sales management officials for assistance with my next sales call was not necessary anymore. The "can-you-help-me-boss?" mentality evaporated.

The Independent Victor Babb Agency Development (IVBAD) Years started when I opened my own Allstate Agency on May 1, 1988 in Elmont, New York. I was again open to new strategies, for I was in a new territory. I attended motivational seminars in order to hear some of the best speakers around the country. My goal was to work on forecasting and planning for my agency.

During my early years, I would work on a marketing strategy for an entire 12-month period. As an agency owner, I still continue this practice. In the Babb Agency we never want to be "played out." I strive to be a solid performer who seeks to make a great income at doing what I do best . . . selling!

The IVBAD Years are superb. I am comfortable calling on bank vice presidents or senior executives. I will only call on my upper management for help in a crisis. I exhibit true professionalism and flexibility. Though I realize that there is still more to learn about selling, I don't worry about it. I am on automatic pilot, confident that my settings are correct and the weather ahead is clear. I expect absolutely no turbulence whatsoever. It's smooth sailing, now! All I have to do is watch my compass occasionally, check my fuel and stay the course. The future is all mapped out. All I have to do is <u>be of service to anybody and everybody and always be ready to serve</u>.

As an insurance executive, the excitement I felt in my early years is still in me. I am enthused with new and bigger ideas and bigger goals. They make me run faster and harder. In fact, they make me run for my life.

Every sales call presents a new opportunity to tap into my brain's database of sales information and human psychology. Thus, my preparation for my next sales call actually began when I was given four insurance manuals to take home in 1974.

As my first sales manager told me, "Victor, you have to know your business so well that every question the prospect brings up, you must know the answer to it."

Now, in the midst of my IVBAD Years, I see things through the eyes of my prospects. I know they are looking at me as a man with a plan. I must tread lightly across the waters of their friendship. I cannot afford for people to falsely think that I am just trying to make a buck. The image I need them to have is of a man who is trying to help his fellow man. I must always seek to help first and sell second.

When I enter the home or office of a prospect, I humbly reflect on my earlier years when I was taught that the first thing I should ask for when entering a home or office is space at a table or desk. This shows the prospect that I want to be comfortable and I will be writing something. Everything I do from that point on—the way I sit; the way I gesture; the way I look at the prospect; the way I breathe—will determine the outcome of the sale.

At the close of every sales call I am thankful, whether the prospect does or does not buy, for I know that I have done my best to sell him or her a brighter tomorrow. I offer all life insurance prospects the same guarantee: to place money in a vault somewhere with his or her name on it; to do in death what they may not have been able to do in life—secure some serious cash for their loved ones.

However, I cannot guarantee how much longer they are going to live. So, after explaining that no other product can substitute for life insurance and that my product is one item that they must buy when they do not need it, I often ask, "Wouldn't it be worth investing a few dollars per month knowing that you are protecting your family and putting your mind at ease?" I have asked this question a thousand times. The answer is always the same. "Yes."

How do you close a sales call with a "Yes"? Remember the importance of the proposal. Whether it is individualized and printed on fine paper or part of a colorful easel display or even purely a verbal proposition, your proposal is your key to making the close. You must buy it first. You must say yes to it first because if *you* don't buy it, you can never sell it. Give the service or product you are selling the power of your emotions. Use the evangelical approach. Believe in it! Believe in it! I beg you to believe in it!

Say Yes to the Sales Call. Find a Way to Close It!

VII

Born to Win

Just as every eagle born is born to fly, every human being born is born to win.

The eagle has captured the imagination of mankind for ages. Perhaps this is because eagles never flock together. They fly with complete freedom. When they see a storm coming, they do what is necessary to weather it. These graceful birds ascend to spectacular heights, higher and farther than any other birds. They are the most majestic birds in the sky.

Nothing stops the eagle from rising above.

Certain individuals obtain the persona of an eagle by soaring to the highest pinnacles of achievement. When they wake up in the morning, they say to themselves, "I am an Eagle. I must fly high."

When they discover the Golden Eagle Spirit within themselves, they wake up and say, "I am a Golden Eagle. I must fly highest."

History has given the world special people who have tapped into their Golden Eagle Spirit. One such illustrious person was Mohandas Gandhi. Revered as the Mahatma, or great soul,

Gandhi made India proud to have him as her son. This late Great Citizen of the second most populous country in the world was a most astounding example of the best that civilization can produce.

He made no money. He did not own a closet full of clothes, but he had real power. How did he gain power? He created it out of his understanding of the principle of faith and through his ability to transplant that faith into the minds of his fellow countrymen. In his mind, there were no limitations. When others disagreed with him, he stood firmly on his convictions. He was a true Golden Eagle.

The climb to the top is never easy in any profession, but it's particularly difficult for a life insurance agent. There are so many negatives that overshadow the agent, he or she has no choice but to develop the self-confidence and self-esteem to stick out his or her chest and announce to the world: "I am a life insurance agent, and I'm proud of it! Just as Mahatma Gandhi was proud to be who he was, I am proud to be who I am."

To the Eagle insurance agents of today, such pride comes naturally. They are already prepared for tomorrow and are excited about their future. They are alert to change. They understand that most industry and government changes are favorable to their business. The successful Eagle agents see an increasing respect for financial planners like themselves and they are capable of handling complex portfolios. They know that behind them is an industry unlike any other in history. These high-flying birds know that they bring better lives to their clients because huge reserves generated by insurance sales are invested in the free market economy to stimulate free enterprise.

Most importantly, Eagle agents and brokers believe that they were born at the right time and in the right place, for they are fully aware that as the world continues to creep towards a new millennium, consumers will appreciate and need even more tailor-made services offered by the insurance professional.

Seeking to dramatize the impressive image of the eagle, Allstate executives started the Golden Eagles club for top life insurance sales producers several years ago in California. Curiously, the New York chapter was started as a result of a bold challenge that I made among my colleagues. I feel comfortable making bold statements because of the many speeches that I have made during my lifetime—speeches such as the one I delivered in the presence of the President of Guyana, Dr. Cheddi Jagan, in 1993.

Poised and self-assured, I ignited the Allstate agents and executives with an idea that had come to me seemingly out of nowhere. We were on the beachhead of Montauk Yacht Club on Long Island, NY. With the savory taste of fresh lobster juice oozing down my throat, I parked myself in a chair across from an agent I did not know. I would soon discover that she was the agent who had been making headlines and creating quite a stir with her life insurance sales production. In fact, some agents had called me days earlier to ask whether I knew her. Not yet realizing who she was, I asked her, "Have you met this new star, Cecille Sassman? She must be quite a woman."

"I am Cecille," she replied.

Towards what I thought was going to be the end of our very pleasant conversation, I challenged her to increase her life insurance sales by 150 percent for the remainder of that year. Just then, the Regional Vice President joined the conversation.

Other managers and agents joined in as well. The R.V.P. said that he liked what he was hearing and challenged all of us to hit the target.

The next morning at our scheduled round-table meeting, the original agenda was scrapped to accommodate the continuation of the previous evening's lobster feast chat. We realized that the energy we were generating was good for the company and good for us as individuals as well. What we needed now was a way to channel the energy into a specific direction.

Shortly after that meeting, Vince Fusco, the Territorial Agency Manager (who is now a R.V.P) requested that I help him put together a group of agents like myself to form a "Golden Eagles" club. He said, "Victor, I can think of only about a dozen or so out of 160 agents in my market who would qualify. I'll ask the Sales Vice President to come in and formally give the club his blessings."

On January 31, 1996, sure enough, Chuck Martin, the S.V.P., came to the first meeting of the Golden Eagles club and cut the ribbon so that fourteen members could commence with the growth and development of the fledgling enterprise. On February 8th, Frank Brady, Territorial Education Manager, visited my office to officially request that I become the Golden Eagles's first Chairman. At the second meeting a month later, with the steering committee in place, I was confirmed to serve as chairman. I accepted the appointment.

As my first official action I suggested that another club be created to serve as a springboard to help other (smaller producing) agents increase their sales and qualify for entry into the Golden Eagles club. This springboard club would be called the Eagles. My idea was accepted. I was glad to know that the idea of forming a superior life insurance sales club was becoming more than just a short-lived topic of a shop talk session.

The first Golden Eagles club meeting was held with 35 agents who met the requirements for charter membership. After the R.V.P., opened the breakfast meeting with brief remarks, he quickly turned the floor over to me for my input.

Addressing the audience, I said, "Good morning. A former President of the United States once said, 'Ask not what your country can do for you, ask what you can do for your country.' I would like to turn that statement around by saying this: ask not what your company can do for you, ask what you can do for your company.

"Sir Winston Churchill, of England, once said, 'Success is never final; never get elated over a win; when you lose, you must find the lesson in it.'

"The great Civil Rights leader, the Rev. Dr. Martin Luther King Jr., who was assassinated in Memphis, Tennessee, said during one of his famous speeches, 'If a man has nothing for which to die, he is not fit to live.'

"When I challenged Cecille to a higher level of production, I meant every word of it. I left that meeting in Montauk ready to fulfill my promise to increase my sales production. I went back to my office and made a blue print for the next six months of the year and then I worked tirelessly to guarantee that I would be No. 1.

"Number one is something that I always wanted to be in the insurance business—not just in my district or territory—but in an entire region.

"Sometime ago I was down on the island of Barbados. I stopped to help an old man walk across the street. He said to me, 'You know, life down here is like going through a horn pipe.'

"I replied, 'What do you mean?'

"He responded, 'A horn pipe is a small pipe and, if you can get anything through there, you are good.'

"Sometimes selling life insurance can be like going through a horn pipe . . . The R.V.P. is sitting here looking like he is the owner of a large aircraft company with all of these big jets ready to take off. Perhaps, I can help them with their liftoff by sharing my 24 steps to success. These steps empowered me to successfully reach my revised goal in just six short months last year:" Then I shared with them the following success tips:

Victor Babb's 24 Steps to Success

1. Put God first.
2. Put family second and career third.
3. Be sure to follow your heart, for it is as dependable as a compass.
4. We are all born with a secret to our success. Find out what it is and use it. And do not quit.
5. Set your own time frame to begin your own race. Do not let anyone set that time frame for you.
6. Listen to highly effective motivational tapes in your car.
7. Spend less time with unproductive people.
8. Read everything that you can get your hands on, if it pertains to your career and your goals.
9. Expand your biological family into a larger circle of adopted family. Let them know that they are part of your family.

10. Schedule vacations or retreats so as to maintain your sanity; meet new people with new ideas; recharge your energy and, most of all, avoid burn out and conformity. Travel to different places.
11. Buy something for yourself after each significant victory, but only if you think you did your very best during the contest.
12. Involve your staff in all of your goals. Always find a way to reward your staff early.
13. Rearrange your priorities constantly in response to significant unexpected developments.
14. Think, dress, talk and act as a successful person at all times.
15. If you want money, help someone to get something they need. Remember, the best way to help yourself is to help someone else.
16. Always set achievable goals and never quit because the moment you stop trying is the moment you fail.
17. Periodically remind yourself about your background, your qualifications and your experience. These form the springboard for your ultimately successful efforts to reach your goals. Consider these as reminders or personal pep talks.
18. Write down the names of the people on whose shoulders you are going to stand in order to achieve your objectives.
19. Pick out a few private or public personalities that you know you are smarter or better than, and then prove it to the world.
20. The world is a stage and you are a player in the band,

thus always present your best performance.
21. Never wait for next year, for it may never come.
22. Always be prepared to solve a problem before it becomes your own. You must have a plan.
23. Have a weekly exercise schedule; decrease your leisure time. Keep your attitude adjusted.
24. Finally, pray, aspire, smile and run your life as you desire. <u>For, ultimately, you are your own boss!</u>

"To sum this all up, my fellow agents, let your motto be 'Always forward, never backward.' Thank you for listening to me."

Jerry Choate, Allstate Chairman and CEO, spoke at the next meeting of these high-flying Eagles. Before he spoke, I presented remarks: "Mr. Chairman," I said, "I have not personally met you before today. I have known you only by your reputation. By reputation you are a workaholic. Well, if you are going to work yourself to death, there's no better cause than for the people."

At the end of his speech, there were questions and further remarks. Afterwards, he sat down next to me on the dais and whispered, "Victor, in 10 years you are going to be very proud of this club."

Two weeks later I was elected president of the Golden Eagles club. The club quickly became a household name within the agency ranks. Now, I regularly receive telephone calls from managers asking me to present sales ideas and techniques to their sales teams.

The focus of my presentations is usually *The Value and Marketing of Life Insurance.* Agents are asked to come with questions and ideas. The printed invitations to my presentations state: *It Is About Making Money . . . Making Lots Of Money!* "

One of the presentations was held in Yonkers, NY. I was particularly delighted to be there. As I told the agents, "I am happy to visit with you again, after leaving here 12 years ago. I am indeed honored to come before you this morning. This is like a rebirth, and I owe it to your flamboyant and distinguished agency manager, Les Vixama. When he asked me to speak today, I immediately seized the opportunity so that I could see some of you who I have personally hired and managed in the past. Seeing here so many old friends, I am tempted to talk of years gone by.

"But I am not here this morning to dwell on the past. Not that the past isn't useful; it sharpens perspective, warns of pitfalls and helps to point the way to the future. But we must never let it divert our attention from the present. So let us move down the stretch and talk about why I am here. My subject this morning is *The Value and Marketing of Life Insurance.*

"Let us consider your basic role as an agent for a moment. You sell to a wide range of a clientele, both individuals and businesses. You sell face-to-face in situations that demand your involvement in the wants and needs of your clients. You must prepare life insurance plans that require you to make judgments. These judgments are often based on evaluations that are not found in a rate book, sales manual or computer. They have to do with measuring the dreams of your client, sizing up the very tangible factor of how much your client can afford and then gauging how much the client is willing to pay. Every selling situation is different; sometimes we have to go with our instincts.

"I get a high when my fellow agents let me know how well

I have done. Here is one such letter that I received from an agent: 'Hey, Vic, just a note to tell you that I'm happy for your great success, not only last year, but during your entire career with Allstate. It is very motivating. You're smart, a hard worker and a determined go-getter. But more than that, when you took time out to share in my moment of grief, when my mother passed away, it meant a great deal to me. It showed me your depth of character. Hey guy, good job. Good show! You make us proud. Hearty congratulations on all your success. May God grant you more, Dan Balizario.'

"Letters and feedback like this keep me going. They keep my wings spread out wide, like an eagle's." I continued: "Let me define one of the biggest words in our vocabulary: success. You must do a job so well that the next person cannot do it any better. Success is in the way you walk the paths of life each day. Success is being big of heart, clean, and broad of mind. Success is being faithful to your friends and to the stranger. Success is in the family that you love. Success is having character in everything you do . . . Let your results be outstanding and I will see *you* at the top!

"Let me share with you what I consider to be the ten hottest tips for the Golden Eagles club:

Golden Eagle Top Ten Tips

"As David Letterman would say, at number . . .

"10: The Golden Eagles club is built on trust. The club is about getting your average premium higher. Working your current processes to get more.

"9. At times you need to talk to a positive agent. Pick one

to be your running buddy. You will have a lot of fun.

"8. One agent said, he calls selling life insurance, 'The Big Chase.' It takes persistency, but the rewards are great, especially the bonuses.

"7. Get involved and get acquainted with the industry products. Get CLU (Chartered Life Underwriter) and LUTC (Life Underwriter Training Council). Get educated.

"6. We should bring in other agents as speakers and other successful business people.

"5. Make sure we, the Golden Eagles, run the club and the friendship will develop. Remember, this is about commitment and consistency.

"4. Selling is about offering a service that you know your prospect needs and then helping the prospect find the money, no matter what the prospect tells you.

"3. Stay among people who are upbeat, not jaded.

"2. You might not like it, but do it anyway, until you reach your goal. Then you will like it just fine. I once heard a determined Eagle agent say, for eight weeks last year all he did was write life insurance, though he did not like to do it. But, he smiled and said, 'I got over it.'

"And my No. 1 selling idea for the Golden Eagles is: selling life insurance is like a deck of cards. Pull one name off of your list and ask somebody to buy a policy."

The audience loved this entertaining technique. As they heartily applauded, I smiled, paused, took a sip of water and then resumed my presentation, which lasted 90 minutes:

"Let me share with you four letters I received: 'March 29, 1996. Dear Victor, your outstanding accomplishments in 1995 have earned you special recognition at our 1996 Chairman's Conference. What a fantastic year! Congratulations to our No. 1 Golden Eagle. Regards, Michael E. Brown, Territorial Agency Manager.'

"'Dec. 13. 1996. Dear Victor, just a note to say thank you very much for the invitation to join your Golden Eagles meeting last Monday. I sure enjoyed the opportunity to meet with your team during lunch and for the business portion of your session. It was great to see the well deserved recognition of the members of your Golden Eagles club. In addition to saying thanks, I would also like to congratulate you, Victor, and all of your team members for the leadership you are displaying in the New York Metro Region. Efforts like yours will continue to support the significantly improving life insurance results that are occurring in New York Metro. Obviously, such results are beneficial to the region and to the agents who make it happen.

"'However, most important of all, increased life sales results mean we are doing better at serving our customers. We are offering them the protection they and their families need. Once again, thanks for your results. Best regards, Joseph P. McFadden, Territorial Vice President.'

"The next letter is from an agent who I helped open a new office: 'Jan. 29, 1997. Dear Victor, one can only judge the content of one's efforts by the end results, and the results are outstanding. I must say, thank you with all sincerity because without you I would not have shone as brightly as I did at the kick off. My production would not have excelled as it has. You gave unselfishly, and from the heart, of your friendship, time and knowledge. I accepted and applied your wisdom to produce outstanding results. In the beginning, when I was lost, you took me under your wing and taught me how to fly. Yesterday, because of you, I experienced the joys of soaring among the Eagles. You not only fed me, but groomed me for the future. I will never be able to thank you enough or repay you for your friendship or your work. My gratitude is immeasurable for you were unique and flawless in your dedication to see me succeed. Thank you, from the heart. Beverly Joseph.'

"Recently, I received this note: 'Dear Victor, congratulations on attaining the Life Leader Special Underwriting Program status during 1997! This recognition is reflective of your concern for the protection of the lives of your customers and their families. You are one of only six agents in our territory who have achieved this milestone. Victor, upon reviewing the record book, I realized you are the only agent in the territory to attain Life Leader status for six consecutive years ('92, '93, '94, '95, '96 and '97). That is quite an accomplishment. Congratulations once again and I hope you're able to put your Life Leader stamp to good use! Regards, John A. Kane, Territorial Agency Manager.'"

Shortly after reading John Kane's letter, I ended the presentation. A few days later, I read his letter again to myself and reflected deeply on its contents because it reminded me of certain basic principles that undergird my life insurance sales philosophy. In a nutshell, I do not limit myself when selling policies to businesses or individuals. You see, whether I am selling to a business or an individual, the basic needs for life insurance protection are all the same. The client wants to either create capital or conserve capital. Thus, business insurance is personal insurance. This sales perspective has empowered me to keep my sales performance much higher than the norm.

Following this philosophy, I have discovered a gold mine in the business arena, closing Key Person Life Insurance; Corporate Stock Retirement Plans; Partial Stock Retirement Plans for Estate Liquidity and Deferred Compensation Plans.

For the record, I will explain the above-referenced classifications of insurance:

Key Person Life Insurance is insurance purchased by a business firm on the life of an owner or employee whose services contribute substantially to the success of the business.

Corporate Stock Retirement Plans involve several individuals who are joined in the ownership and operation of a closely held business enterprise, such as a closed corporation. The problem of what to do if one member were to die is solved when an insurance policy is put into place to cover any such losses.

Regarding Partial Stock Retirement Plans for Estate Liquidity, it is important to understand that, as a rule, the bulk of a stockholder's estate consists of a business interest. At death, for estate tax purposes, stock is valued but woefully lacking compared to other estate assets that are needed to pay the cost of estate settlement. Therefore, the majority owner of a close corporation will need to be satisfied that the estate will have sufficient liquid assets to pay settlement costs. Without such liquidity, the executor will be forced to dispose of a substantial amount of stock in order to pay estate bills. Unless this is accomplished under a special plan, such stock disposition will destroy the stockholder's hopes for family retention of the business.

A Deferred Compensation Plan provides advantages to both the employer and the executive employee. The employer assures himself or herself of the continuing services and loyalties of key personnel by providing contingent financial rewards to be paid later.

Every eagle is born to see the world from his own perspective, high above the mountains. Only by an eagle's own individual efforts can it ascend to such great heights. Likewise, every human being is born to see his or her own opportunities and to soar to great heights of achievement.

I am blessed to have had the opportunity to mount up with wings and soar to millions of dollars in sales. With the help and encouragement of others, I hope to continue soaring higher and higher—as high as I possibly can.

I hope to see you up there, too.

VIII

Mr. Grandsouldt:
An Eagle for All Seasons

I am convinced that most people living in the United States, no matter how well off or educated, do not understand the plight of the immigrant. In this the greatest country on earth, people often fail to comprehend the nature, the significance and scope of the immigrant's predicament.

Do you have any idea of what it means to leave your native land and take up residence in another man's land? Picture yourself living in an environment void of the comfort of familiar sounds and faces. You are unsure which of the new faces that your apprehensive eyes encounter will be friendly or resentful once the fact that you're an immigrant is revealed.

The difficult American environment, which most immigrants enter voluntarily in their pursuit of life, liberty and happiness, is only made worse by the rampant insensitivity within the American corporate culture. This insensitivity was clearly illustrated in 1995 when one of the world's largest oil companies was caught red-handed, practicing racial discrimination. Texaco Oil Corporation agreed to pay an out-of-court settlement of

$176M to 1,500 of its minority employees. Texaco's chairman of the board, acknowledging that some of his top executives were caught on tape making racist remarks, said that this shameful behavior was only the tip of the iceberg in corporate America. He has since asked his counterparts to work honestly and aggressively towards wiping out racism in their corporations. He further stated that this goal is quite attainable in America, if there is the will to do so.

Until such behavior and attitudes are eliminated, however, the corporate and social environments will continue to create serious pitfalls for the immigrant.

That the Texaco settlement is the largest racial discrimination settlement in U.S. history is a clear indication of how strong you have to be in order to fight racism. Those employees who won the suit demonstrated that you must not just break the glass ceiling in America, you have to down right smash it.

Despite its challenges, America is still a great place to spread your wings, no matter who you are. I know for a fact that America has a built-in system that allows an individual more freedom and rights than most other countries.

These benefits and blessings are actually the fruits of the labors of many who have made awesome sacrifices throughout the years. President Abraham Lincoln and Dr. Martin Luther King, Jr. serve as just two examples of the courage and vision that have both shaped America into what she is and inspired her to continue to strive towards what she can become.

However, there is one little-known man who I admire more than all of the heroes and leaders in American history. He was not American, but he stood for the right of others to pursue life, liberty and happiness. I wish he had been my father, however this man was not related to me at all. His name was Robert Grandsouldt, a Guyanese.

During my teenage years in Guyana, a few of us clean-cut boys, who were very close friends, decided that we would form a networking group called the Magnificent 7. We were very hungry for success, but not at any price. We wanted to make our parents proud of us. So, all of us, Deryck, Robin, Vincent, Maurice, Khan, John and I, depended on our home training to guide us through life.

On one Easter Sunday evening we were having dinner at a restaurant in Georgetown, Guyana, chatting about our big dreams and plans. Suddenly, out of the blue, I asked everyone, "Tell, me: Who is the person you admire the most?"

Silence fell over us as we pondered the question. Even I took time to think of who it was I admired the most, for I had no clear idea, though I was the one who posed the question.

All of us lived in single-parent households. There were no fathers in our homes. It was no surprise, then, that all of us would choose a male role model, but, amazingly, all seven of us chose the same father figure as the best example for us to follow—Robert Grandsouldt.

Except for Maurice, we all worked for the Guyana Graphic, the largest newspaper company in the country. We all started out at the bottom of the ladder, while still attending school, working as messenger boys or office boys, just as some of the senior officials in the company had done years before.

Mr. Grandsouldt was one of those top-ranking managers who had been promoted from within the company. To us, he was a hero because he was a young man who only had a high school education, but still rose to the top.

When I joined the company at the age of 16, he was an advertising assistant, aged 34. By the time he hit 40, he was Chief Executive Officer. I watched Grandsouldt make his moves. I will always remember his positive mental attitude and his energy. He wanted to succeed and to bring others along with him. He was always well groomed, both physically and politically. Each time he was promoted, he made it his duty to quickly learn every facet of departmental operations. He was not reluctant to do what another employee would not do. He worked long hours, sometimes returning during the wee hours of the morning to check on the quality of the newspaper run for that day.

He was very decisive, but polite. He always acted like a true professional. He was tough, but fair. He possessed integrity and honesty. He respected every person's opinion. Grandsouldt wanted me and my peers to excel! He was a wise manager, for he realized that, if he gave his subordinates some power, he would eventually have more power.

We proudly called him "Mr. Grandsouldt." Well loved by all who worked for him, he was the role model who you would want for your son or daughter. He did not have great wealth or fame. He was not a political leader. He was not an entertainer. He was not a sports super star, but he knew that success is definitely a game—a mind game—and he was playing to win.

Each member of the Magnificent 7 could see his future self in Mr. Grandsouldt. That is the main reason why we, individually and collectively on that Easter Sunday afternoon, chose Mr. Grandsouldt as the man to watch and admire.

Tragically, he lost his life in an automobile accident after he had conducted some company business and was returning back to his office. We will always remember him for the way he lived, for he left a legacy. He was an Eagle for All Seasons.

Mr. Grandsouldt showed us by example how to take charge and do the right thing. He proved that great leaders are usually ordinary people who have prepared themselves for extraordinary circumstances. On the other hand, the Magnificent 7 proved that every young person has a duty to choose his or her role model and everyone must be careful what role model one chooses.

In choosing Mr. Grandsouldt as our role model, we chose a great elder in our community. Great elders are those individuals who care enough about you to dare *you* to become great. Needless to say, today's youths need more elders like Mr. Grandsouldt.

As an immigrant, I often think of his example as I make my own moves up the ladder of success. Though now a grown man, I realize that the memories of Mr. Grandsouldt still empower me to see what my future can be, thus I never doubt that higher and higher levels of success are possible for me. After all, I am like Mr. Grandsouldt—just an ordinary man who has prepared himself to capitalize on extraordinary opportunities.

Thank you, Mr. Grandsouldt, for showing me the way.

IX

Soaring: From Continent to Continent

Eagles tend to fly far and wide. So do successful people.

Being considered a world-class sales executive affords me the luxury of free trips abroad, where I enjoy the beauty of both nature and mankind and experience a variety of excitement and adventure as well.

Whether my travels are the results of winning free trips for my high performance in sales or whether the trips are financed by myself, I always have a great and splendid time.

During the past 24 years, I have won award after award and traveled about six times a year, being wined and dined in some of the most exotic hotels and restaurants in the world. I have visited 25 countries and 25 states.

As a result of my journeys, I am wiser and I have a much greater appreciation for my freedom. I am grateful that hard work does have its rewards, especially if you work with the right people—and even more so if you work in sales. So, the next time you hear that someone you know is going into sales, persuade him to go for it! Tell him to give it his blood, sweat and tears! Tell her to give like she never has before, for the rewards are always there to be taken by those who give their all.

Now, allow me to take you on a whirlwind tour with me back through time on some of my favorite trips:

As I stated in an earlier chapter, I won my first trip in 1974. I visited Lake George in upstate New York. This was a thrill, but my second trip felt even better. Travelling from the east to the west coast of the United States in 1975 was like a dream come true. I felt like I had hit the big time. What a far cry from the small boats and the old English yellow school buses back home in Guyana.

I once went to Sydney, Australia for a sales convention. This country now tops my list for genuine hospitality. There I learned that the people make a country beautiful, not the scenery. I spent 10 days there with my daughter, Nicole. It was a lifelong dream of mine to go to the country called "Down Under."

As an example of Australian hospitality, consider this: As my daughter and I were leaving, the hotel bellman took our luggage to the curb. We wondered why he was still standing around talking to us after he had refused our tip. He waited for about 30 minutes before our ride showed up. He said that it was his job to see that all guests leave without a problem.

If I had a chance to return to Australia again and again, I certainly would. If you get a chance to go, remember to visit Blue Mountain. What a sight!

Other great convention sites and tourist destinations were Vienna, Austria; Madrid, Spain and Hong Kong, China. How sweet they were.

Africa and The Middle East

Africa is the one place that you must visit, if you consider yourself a world traveler.

Nigeria is one of the largest countries in the world. With more than one hundred million people, it is considered the China of Africa. Plan to spend at least two weeks, if you go. While on my trek, my plane touched down in Ghana for a few hours en route to Lagos. I walked toward the open back door of the plane to take in the cool breeze coming off the Sahara Desert. The wind welcomed me and reminded me that I am a son of Africa. From somewhere on this vast continent came my ancestors.

On July 5, 1997 I went on a mission to Israel and Egypt. This trip was organized by Wilberforce University, in Ohio. Going to the Middle East was not a vacation. It was a serious journey, a personal discovery of the inner secrets of my religion.

Israel left the deepest impression on me because it is the Land of Jesus, best known as the Holy Land. After arriving at Ben Gurion Airport, I traveled to many historic sites, including Bethlehem, Calvary, the Dead Sea, the Garden of Gethsemane, the Garden Tomb, the Golan Heights, Nazareth, the River Jordan, the Sea of Galilee and the Wailing Wall, just to name a few.

My spiritual awareness and knowledge of the Bible were greatly enhanced by my visit to the Holy Land. Words cannot describe this experience. If you want to know what I am talking about, just go!

A fascinating journey through time awaits visitors to ancient Egypt. I had the pleasure of visiting Cairo and the great Egyptian

Museum. Of course, I cruised the Nile and visited the Pyramids at Giza and took in the awesome Evening Pyramid Sound and Light show, replete with sound effects and dramatic narrations.

These are just a few samples of my journeys. Traveling will always be an essential part of my life because it is full of surprises, and encountering the unexpected keeps me feeling alert and young. Whenever I need instant motivation to continue working hard, all I have to do is envision my next fascinating trip. I can't wait to go!

Epilogue

My sole intention for writing this book was to impart my tenets of success to all who care to know.

I hope that within these pages you have found inspiration, hope, determination and some spirituality. What I have stated in this book is not simply what I believe to be true. It is what I know to be true, for this has been the story of what I have personally experienced.

The ultimate satisfaction from writing this book will come when people like you, who, after reading it and sharing it with others, will appreciate what it truly means to be your own Golden Eagle.

If tonight's news is of the "imminent end of the world," let it be known that I am an eternal optimist. The positive things that have occurred in my life compel me to be no less than 100 percent optimistic. I contend that this book, while not a panacea for all things negative, can help anyone—adults and children in all walks of life—to become more positive and therefore more happy, productive and successful.

Of course, he or she who aspires to be the best must be quite willing to pay the price. Thus, I challenge you to choose a direct course towards a life full of excitement and joy and never stray from it, despite the odds.

Remember, no matter what, your life is worth living to the fullest. So, by all means, direct your energies towards experiencing all that life has to offer.

The most valuable benefits of life are intangible. Go inside to find them. Once you caress them deep within your soul, all else becomes pleasurable—or at least bearable.

As for me, something within makes me want to soar—from openings to closings, from continent to continent, from one interesting person to the next, enjoying life and taking in the sights and sounds of the world.

The higher I soar, the more I am glad that I accepted the greatest challenges of my life:

The challenge of becoming a person of vision.

The challenge of becoming somebody special.

The challenge of becoming a Golden Eagle.

The challenge of being free!

And I thank God Almighty for giving me the desire and the courage to accept the challenge to be as free as I can possibly be!

Every day of my life I strive to meet these challenges.

I hope that you will accept these challenges too.

I am a man.
I am somebody . . .